Becoming a

BETTER
PARENT

Maurice Balson
MONASH UNIVERSITY

Hodder & Stoughton

TOR ONTO

ISBN 0 340 51009 9

First published by The Australian Council for Educational
Research Ltd., Radford House, Frederick Street, Hawthorn,
Victoria 3122, Australia.

Copyright © Maurice Balson 1981, 1987

This edition first published in the United Kingdom in 1989.

Printed and bound in Great Britain for
the educational publishing division of
Hodder and Stoughton Ltd,
Mill Road, Dunton Green, Sevenoaks, Kent by
Biddles Ltd, Guildford and King's Lynn

Contents

Introduction

The excellent reception given to the first edition of *Becoming Better Parents* by parents and professionals, has encouraged me to prepare a second edition. The basic purpose of the book remains the same: to make available to parents, a psychological approach to understanding children and to describe a set of principles which may be used by parents in their daily experiences with children in homes and families.

The book remains organised around the work of Alfred Adler and the framework offered by Individual Psychology. The second edition incorporates two new sections, adolescence and single-parent families. The demand for material on adolescence has been heavy and it is apparent that many parents are experiencing problems with their adolescent age children. The problems of drugs, alcohol, reckless driving and delinquency appear to have worsened in teenagers in recent years and an attempt is made in the new chapter on adolescents to provide parents with approaches which they may find effective.

The single-parent family has now become firmly established as part of our culture. The single-parent family includes widowed, divorced, separated, adopted, and never married — all representing alternative family systems rather than 'broken homes'. Although the initial problem faced by single-parent families are those related to the event which created their particular status, in time, the problems of those families begin to resemble those of the more traditional family. However, parents from single-parent families have a number of unique problems and their requests for assistance have prompted the inclusion of a special chapter on specific techniques which are valuable for single parents.

All of the original chapters have been revised in light of changing social conditions and specific comments and feedback received from parents. As with the first edition, the second edition places a great emphasis on the application of the psychological framework and principles to the wide range of typical situations and problems encountered in the family. Conflict resolution approaches have also been included.

The book shares the philosophy of Alfred Adler and Rudolf Dreikurs who believe that the improvement of the child is in direct correlation to the improvement in the parent. Because the individual's personality is formed in the first few years of life, the early years are crucial for the well-being of the child and, subsequently, for the person in adulthood. 'Parent education is thus vital, since future difficulties can be prevented when parents learn to raise their children in line with Adlerian principles'. (Ferguson, 1984) It is to 'becoming a better parent' that this book is directed.

If we are to have better children,
parents must become better educators.

Rudolf Dreikurs

1
A New Tradition of Child Raising

Lack of Tradition in Child Raising

An upsurge in public interest in the problems of family living and in child raising reflects many people's concern regarding the perplexing problem of children's behaviour. Seldom has an adult generation expressed such vital interest in, and at the same time concern for, a younger generation. Dreikurs (1959:18) justifies this concern when he notes: 'The obvious reason for our predicament is the lack of tradition in raising children. Today's parents simply do not know what to do with them.'

The lack of tradition referred to above needs explaining. Child raising has followed a definite pattern which parents and children alike clearly understood. Each generation passed on to the next those parenting techniques which have been proven effective over time, and well-defined patterns were established for meeting typical life situations and conflicts.

The Autocratic Parent

The characteristic methods of raising children were based on an autocratic society, a phase of society which began with our civilisation about eight thousand years ago. In an autocratic society, one group established its superiority over another and accepted the responsibility for deciding the behavioural patterns of those in the inferior group. This superior-inferior continuum applied to parent-child, male-female, white-coloured, management-labour and teacher-student relationships. Traditionally, parents made all decisions concerning children's behaviour. 'You will get up when I tell you to get up. You will go to bed when I tell you to go. You will eat what I tell you to eat. You will toilet-train when I tell you to toilet-train. You will wear what I tell you to wear.' Similarly, males decided the behaviour of females, white dominated coloured and teachers controlled the behaviour of students.

Within this superior-inferior relationship, born of an autocratic society, parents were in no doubt about how to raise their children. They decided exactly how each child would behave and used rewards and punishments to enforce compliance. In other words, they used exactly the same methods of raising their children as their own parents used. By rewarding a child, the parents communicated a clear message: 'Because you have done what I wanted you to do, I will reward you.' Punishment indicated the same lack of respect: 'Because you have not done what I wanted you to do, I will punish you.'

The task of being a parent was not difficult — decide what you want the child to do or not to do, and use the threat of punishment or the promise of reward to induce compliance. This approach was very successful and many parents reported that they had very 'co-operative' children, a reference to the fact that the children did exactly what the parents wanted the children to do. Co-operation meant simply doing as you were told.

As long as the autocratic society remained stable, this approach to raising children was effective and each generation of parents learned the techniques from their own parents. Parenting courses, lectures on understanding children, books on raising children, newspapers and magazine articles on parenting and radio talk-back sessions on children were unnecessary. Parents knew how to raise their children. Suddenly the whole situation changed and today an entire generation of parents is uncertain of how to raise their children responsibly.

Breakdown of Traditional Parenting Approaches

Our generation of parents is confronted with a changed society which has rendered their traditional methods of raising children obsolete, yet they do not know newer and more effective approaches. The typical home provides ample evidence of the breakdown of our traditional approaches for influencing children. Increasing numbers of parents complain of their inability to understand the behaviour of their children, while children act in such a way as to render parenthood a more difficult task. Parents are unable to get children out of bed in the morning without several reminders; the universal hunger drive has been lost in young children as parents urge and coax them to eat; squabbling between members of a family has become so common that it is accepted as normal — a recent study showed that 75 per cent of homes have a fight before breakfast! It would seem that this is the first generation of parents who do not know how to raise their children. What has given rise to their uncertainty?

The problem facing parents is part of a world-wide movement which has its roots in the social revolution of our times. In essence, parents are products of one type of social system while their children are products of another. The two respective social systems are autocratic and democratic, and the principles of child raising appropriate to each are incompatible.

In our own time, we have seen the collapse of the autocratic social system and the acceptance of a democratic approach to human relationships. The changes came quickly and their results were devastating for all branches of society. With their traditional techniques of raising children rendered ineffective by these vast social upheavals, parents face the dilemma of not knowing what to do with their children and of having little available help which is attuned to the new democratic society in which we live.

From an Autocratic to a Democratic Society

The collapse of the autocratic system started to become evident after World War II and was seen in movements such as Women's Liberation, Black Power, Student Power, and more recently in the high incidence of industrial strife. Each of these movements was motivated by a common resolve, the refusal of one group to accept a position of inferiority. Coloured demanded to be treated as equal with whites; women refused to accept the inferior status accorded them by men; students demanded a greater degree of freedom and autonomy in their education, while labour declined to be dominated by management. Realising that parents could no longer *force* them to do anything, children sought to establish their equality with parents, a demand that met with considerable support and success — hence the dilemma facing parents.

Parents are aware of their responsibility for raising children but many still cling to traditional and ineffective methods of doing so. Consequently, many parents feel frustrated and defeated when these methods do not work and so a vicious cycle is set up. Driven by a sense of responsibility, parents cannot tolerate defeat in this area

which, to many, is their most important task. They become afraid
of the possible tragic consequences that may result if they cannot
control their children. Therefore, they demand submissive acceptance of their requests for what they regard as proper behaviour.
Parents are unaware that they are acting not in the child's interest
but in the interest of their own badly shattered authority. Thus, as
they increase their demand for obedience, children increase their
rebellion and defiance.

Parents' traditional approaches to raising children which came
from an autocratic society are no longer valid. Domination, the use
of rewards and punishments, and pressure from above simply meet
with increased resistance by children. Knowing no other approach,
many parents are bankrupt in their dealings with children. The
more they try to make a child behave in a certain way, the more
defiant, disobedient, and stubborn the child becomes. It is apparent
that defiance and outright rebellion, normally characteristics of
adolescence, are being found now in very young children.*

The eternal smouldering conflict between the generations which
was in the past contained by the power of the adult authority, now
finds open expression either in subtle forms of behaviour or in full
conflict. Children feel misunderstood and abused while adults feel
defeated and angry.

---

* The author interviewed a mother and a boy of 18 months. When they entered the office, the
child's thumb was in his mouth. When I said to him 'Leave your thumb in your mouth', it was
out in a flash. Tell them what to do and they are bound to do the opposite.

Nature of Social Equality

Consider the concept of 'equality' which has become a dominant value in our society. What does it mean to say that women have obtained a position of social equality with men, coloured with whites, or children with their parents? It means simply the right of self-determination, to decide one's own values, behaviours, and future. There is no suggestion that children are as wise, experienced, strong, or knowledgeable as their parents, yet they do have the right to self-determination. Why is it that whites have stopped telling coloured how to behave? Because they do not have the right to do so. Similarly, men no longer prescribe women's behaviour because they also do not have the right. Parents are now learning that they are in a similar position. It is important to realise that the only person for whom one is totally responsible is oneself. While parents have a responsibility and an obligation to provide guidance and leadership for their children, they do not have the right to impose their beliefs and values on children. To do so violates the concept of respect, a crucial value in a democratic society.

Conflict between Parents and Children

The deep concern for children felt by parents often forces them into inappropriate action. In their mistaken belief that children will not improve without adult influence, parents force their children into

inferior roles, thereby creating the seeds of dissension. The consequences are only too apparent. Children refuse to eat, refuse to go to
bed, refuse to tidy up, refuse to pick up belongings, refuse to stop
fighting, and so on. Parents, believing they know what is right,
attempt to impose on, or dominate children. Conflict is inevitable.
The demand 'You get up when I tell you' or 'You will eat what I tell
you to eat' will be met by equally strong responses that say 'I will
get up when I am ready to get up' or 'I will eat what I want to eat'.
Do we have the right to make children behave in certain ways? Are
we sure we know what is right? Can we really make a child do
anything? Is it the need of children for adequate rest, sound
nutrition, or sensible TV viewing which is at stake, or is it really the
desire of the parents that children will do as they are told? Once the
spirit of co-operation is broken and the contest begins, there is no end
to it. There is no final victory possible and the vicious circle continues
as parents and children try to impose their ways on the other.

The need for the child to establish acceptable behavioural patterns
in society is indisputable. The manner in which this is achieved is
critical. To stimulate children into desirable ways of behaving by
using methods which are based on mutual respect, co-operation,
trust, shared responsibility, and social equality is the task facing
parents and the objective to which this book is addressed. While
these methods are discussed in relation to children, they are equally
valid in all relationships between people.

Freedom and Order

It would be a mistake to assume that permissiveness is being advocated. Far from it. While our traditional autocratic techniques resulted in order, there was no freedom for children at all. They did exactly what they were told. With the advent of a democratic climate, many parents wrongly assumed that they should simply stop being autocratic. Children were given freedom, and order was disregarded. The results were disastrous, as chaos and anarchy characterised our homes, schools, and society. It is impossible to have freedom without order, a lesson which was learnt the hard way in the 1960s and 1970s.

A democratic home is characterised by both freedom and order. While children have more freedom today than in previous generations, they have not been taught to use it wisely. How can they learn when parents accept the responsibility for children's behaviour and children are free to do as they wish? There is no point in respecting order when you are shielded from the consequence of being disorderly. Responsibility cannot be learned if you are not required to experience the consequences of irresponsibility. Parents need to learn that all behaviour has a consequence and that allowing children to experience the consequence of their behaviour is the most powerful of all training techniques. The child has *freedom* to choose and will experience the consequences of any behaviour which violates *order*. For example, the child who gets up late (freedom) will experience the consequences at school (order). The child who does not eat (freedom) becomes hungry (order). A child who prefers to kick a football until 8 p.m. misses out on dinner. Freedom (the child's decision to play late) is combined with order ('I am sorry that you missed dinner') to provide learning experiences from which the child will learn responsible behaviours, not because he has been made to behave by the use of rewards or punishments, but because he has experienced the consequences when he violates order.

It is in the development of responsibility in children, that parents make their greatest mistakes. Possessing a strong need to be good parents, they view irresponsible behaviour in children as evidence that they are failing as parents. Consequently they involve themselves in more of the children's responsibilities such as dressing, homework, putting things away and eating. By becoming more responsible, parents teach their children to be less responsible. To develop in children the necessary degree of responsibility while granting them their right of freedom is the challenge facing parents.

Try these

(1) Read the following examples of parental behaviour. Which are autocratic and which are democratic?

Behaviour of parent	Autocratic	Democratic
1 I know you like the colour but it would not look nice on you.		✓
2 That's not the way I told you to set the table.	✓	
3 You will really have to work harder at school.	✓	
4 Who agreed to do the dishes tonight?	✓	
5 Here is the 20p for raking up the leaves.	✓	
6 Let's see if we can think of a way of improving your billy-cart.		✓
7 I don't want to hear you using that word again.	✓	
8 I wonder if someone would like to help me tidy up the lounge room.		✓

Hint: Autocratic — pressure from outside the child.
Democratic — stimulation from within the child.

(2) Which of the following situations are designed to teach children respect for order yet, at the same time, allow them to exercise their freedom of choice?

Situation	Order without freedom	Freedom without order	Freedom with order
1 It is now 8 p.m. Go to bed this minute.	✓		✓
2 I know you don't like to eat at 7.30 a.m. I will cook your breakfast later when you would like it.		✓	✓
3 I am sorry that you missed dinner John but dinner is served at 7 p.m.			✓
4 Now that you have slept in so long, I will have to drive you to school or you will be late.		✓	✓

5 If you don't get up this minute, you can forget about the picnic on Sunday.

6 I am sorry that you were late for school but you know what to do about it.

Answers

(1)

Behaviour	Autocratic	Democratic
1	/	
2	/	
3	/	
4		/
5	/	
6		/
7	/	
8		/

(2)

Situation	Order without freedom	Freedom without order	Freedom with order
1	/		
2		/	
3			/
4		/	
5	/		
6			/

2
Psychological Principles for Understanding Children

Introduction

Many parents have difficulty in understanding their children's behaviour which often appears to be illogical and senseless. A boy who fights with his sister may be spoken to, punished, or deprived of privileges such as watching television, pocket money, or special outings; yet he will continue to fight with his sister.

The great differences between children within the same family is another source of bewilderment for most parents. Alice is co-operative, pleasant, tidy, and does well at school. Tim is unco-operative, untidy, unpleasant, and does poorly at school. 'How can they be so different? We treat them both the same', bemoan the parents who will never understand the behaviour of their son and will assume his very different personality is an accident of birth.

To understand children and to foster their physical, intellectual, social, and emotional development requires that parents have a knowledge of human behaviour so that they can make appropriate decisions about their children and can behave in ways which are designed to stimulate their development. The personality theory reflected in this book stems from the work of Alfred Adler and is referred to as Individual Psychology. It is a view of people which recognises them as active decision makers, as purposeful and goal-oriented individuals, relatively free to determine their own behaviour, understood only within their social environment, and unified and consistent in all of their behaviour.

Other views on the nature of people exist. Some see them as passive products of their environment, motivated by unconscious forces such as sex and aggression. The influence of heredity is seen as a major determinant of behaviour by others while the behavioural school believes that personality can be shaped at will by controlling the consequences of an individual's behaviour. The view of the individual as a bundle of needs is not uncommon, and behaviour or personality is viewed as the child's typical way of satisfying these needs.

It serves no purpose to argue the relative strengths and weaknesses of the respective positions. The fact that Individual Psychology has been chosen reflects the writer's belief that it offers the most worthwhile, effective, and acceptable approach for parents who must raise their children in a relatively new social environment, an environment which has already rendered ineffective many of the traditional techniques associated with child raising.

The following principles provide a framework for parents to understand the behaviour of their children. They will be referred to frequently throughout the book and their knowledge is essential for dealing with the typical problems which parents will face in raising their children.

What Motivates Children's Behaviour?

Our view of children is that they are primarily social beings and everything they do is directed at finding their place in groups which are important to them. The desire to belong, to be accepted, to contribute, is the basic motivation behind all behaviour. In the family setting, we can understand a child's behaviour only if we view such behaviour as the child's attempt to be recognised, to feel important, to belong. The extent to which children feel that they belong to the family will determine their willingness to function constructively and co-operatively within the family. It is a sense of inadequacy, a feeling that one cannot belong through constructive activity, which is at the root of all failures, deficiencies, and problem behaviours. In our society, which is so competitive, and characterised by superior-inferior relationships, many children do not have a chance to feel an equal with others and will pursue unsatisfactory ways of belonging, guided by the conclusion that 'I am not good enough'.

Children do not grow up in isolation. All of their behaviours such as language, play, emotions, and skills are learnt and developed in social situations such as the home, the school, and the community. All human problems are social problems. As a result, these behaviours can be understood only if viewed in terms of the social context in which they are acquired. Young children cannot be considered apart from their family while school behaviour has the classroom as its reference point. Adler has stated this position concisely: 'Individual Psychology regards and examines the individual as socially embedded. We refuse to recognise and examine an isolated human being.'

There is nothing more important in life than a child's original family for it is there that the basis of personality is formed. In their transactions within the family, children form ideas about life, themselves and others, ideas which will form the guiding principles throughout life. When families can develop an atmosphere which permits children to experience a sense of belonging to the family, then maladjustment and pathology will not occur. It is only when children feel that they belong successfully to the family, that they will move on in life contributing, participating, and co-operating.

From infancy on, the small child seeks to find those ways of behaving which will gain recognition, feelings of importance, and a sense of belonging to the family. Young children operate on a trial-and-error basis. In their early attempts to seek answers to the questions, 'Who am I? What am I? Who are these people about me? What can I do? How can I belong?', children will try various ways of behaving and observe the consequences. When a child cries, mother comes; she is controlled. Father does not hear crying but will come when the child holds her breath until she is blue in the face. Almost anything works with grandparents who are constantly hovering over the child. Each experience is evaluated by the child: 'Ah, that's how I can keep mother busy with me; that's how I can be noticed; those are the things parents like me to do or try to prevent me from doing; that's how I can belong.' This search for significance and for a place in the family is basic to every child. As each member of the family is both an actor and reactor, there is no one individual who is totally influential. A family is a dynamic process in which each member reacts to others and prompts reaction in them.

Those behaviours which 'work', in that they give a child a sense of belonging, are continued while others which do not achieve this purpose are discontinued. It is not necessary that the behaviours be constructive or socially acceptable; they may be disruptive, unacceptable or foolish from a parent's viewpoint. The only criterion which determines if the behaviour will persist or not is whether it satisfies the child's need to belong, to be noticed, or to feel important.

View Behaviour within the Family

The importance of viewing behaviour within the social context of the family also implies that all corrective efforts by parents in relation to children must be conducted within the environment provided by the total family. A great mistake which parents make is to deal with children in isolation, in a one-to-one situation. For example, if one child is particularly difficult in that he or she fights frequently, declines to eat, or refuses to do what is asked, most parents will talk to the child about this misbehaviour, seek assurances regarding future improvement, or resort to punishment. These approaches completely miss the point. The fact that the behaviour is meaningful within the family setting implies that it can only be developed or corrected within the same setting. By observing children in their relationship to other members of the family, we can begin to understand the purpose for their behaviour and can consider ways in which the members of the family can begin to change the children's behaviour by changing their own.

To demonstrate the importance of involving the total family rather than individual family members, consider the following situation. A family has three children: Jane eight, George seven, and Sally five. Mother and father are divorced and the children live with the mother. Jane is doing well at school, is helpful at home, and assists in every way she can. Would you like to predict the likely behaviours of George? Do you think that he will be similar to Jane or quite different? In all probability, he will do poorly at school and at home will be unco-operative, fight with his sister, and in many ways resemble a hostile boarder. Why is he likely to be so different from Jane? In George's attempt to find a place in the family, what areas does he observe to be successfully occupied? Scholarship, co-operation, pleasantness, and tidiness are the characteristics of Jane. These are the ways in which she belongs and it is unlikely that George will compete in those fields. Why would he want to? There are many other ways of behaving which will gain him a sense of belonging and through his disturbing behaviours, mother and teacher certainly know that George is around.

What of five-year-old Sally? What ways of belonging are still open to her? There is a strong probability that she will be a cute child, pleasant, happy-go-lucky, and able to put people in to her service by being nice. She will not have the high ambition of her sister or the disturbing ways of her brother but she will find her place by being one whom people like to serve: the charmer. It is impossible to understand the behaviour of any one child in this family without understanding the behaviour of the other two. Each child has chosen a way of belonging largely because of the behaviours of the other — Jane is responsible, George is difficult, and Sally is cute.

Who is the problem in the above family? Most parents would consider that George is the major difficulty and their methods of helping him, among other things, would include private talks. Mother might discuss the importance of doing well at school, the need for more co-operation at home, for less fighting and the like. How effective are these 'little talks'? We know that they will not lead to a change in George's behaviour. 'How many times do I have to tell you?' has been asked a thousand times by a thousand parents. George is not about to give up behaviours which 'work'; his belonging depends on his ability to involve you with him through his disturbing and inadequate behaviour. To change George's behaviour, it would be necessary to change the behaviour of his sisters, particularly Jane. She is the major influence on George's behaviour and any program designed to assist George must include his sisters. Jane feels that she belongs as long as she is the best. As such she will make every attempt to ensure that George is unsuccessful in her chosen areas. How successful she has been can be judged by the complete differences in personalities — George is everything that Jane is not while Sally is what neither of the two are. Always view children within the total family and refuse to deal with them individually.

Another example will conclude this point. Imagine your family consists of two children which generally means that you will have a 'good' child and a 'bad' child. Watch how they co-operate to keep you busy all day. When viewing television, the good child may give the other a swift kick on the foot. No response. A second and a third kick will follow in quick succession until finally the bad child will strike back hard. Mother, on hearing the scream, will go up and ask

that foolish question: 'Who started it?' You must see the implicit agreement which children have on their ways of belonging. In this case they have agreed: 'You get your attention by being good and I will get mine by being bad and that is how we will keep parents busy with us'. If parents attempt to correct their bad child — to improve his/her behaviours — and are successful, then they would find that their good child would become bad. Roles would be reversed in this teeter-totter situation. The family group is the only context in which parents may understand behaviour and is the setting in which inadequate behaviour may be rectified. The means of doing this will be discussed in a later section.

All Behaviour Is Purposeful

We have described people as social beings whose basic motivation is to belong. Children, like all other individuals, have the same desire to belong and their behaviour is directed at satisfying this desire. Consequently, all of their behaviour is purposeful, directed at quite specific goals. When parents indicate that they do not understand a child, what they are saying is, in fact, that they are not aware of the purpose or goal of the child's behaviour. Without an understanding and a knowledge of each child's goal, it is impossible to understand or change behaviour.

No child acts at random. Behind all behaviour there is a clear purpose or goal, a condition which prompted Gordon Allport to write: 'Goal striving is the essence of personality'. Once parents become aware of the purpose behind behaviour, they will see that the behaviour is logical and consistent and that the parents' attempts to change the behaviour usually have the opposite effects. For example, when children fight, most parents will stop the fighting, attempt to adjudicate the dispute, and then punish the guilty one. Parental intervention seldom reduces the frequency of fighting because the purpose of fighting is to involve the parent. Children fight for your benefit and what you are inclined to do is exactly what the children want you to do. George fights to show you that he can do what he likes; Jane fights because she has a protector in the form of mother who will always come to her aid. If parents ignored fighting and left children free to settle their own disputes, the incidence of fighting would decrease. Why? Because it would no longer work, no longer achieve its purpose of involving the parents with the children.

The following incident demonstrates the above point. A mother of seven children complained that her youngest son was always being set upon by the others. 'If it wasn't for me', she said, 'they would nearly kill the little one.' 'How old is your little one?' I asked. 'Seven.' Why is it that the baby of the family is always being hit by the others? Because the youngest child provokes the others until they strike him — the scream, mother's intervention, consolation for the youngest, and punishment for the others — and so the fighting persists. We must act in such a way as to eliminate the intended purpose of fighting. Stay out of children's fights and you remove the purpose of the fighting.

As all human behaviour has a purpose, the key to understanding and correcting a child's behaviour is to identify the purpose and then act in such a way that the behaviour does not achieve its intended goal. The methods of determining the goals of behaviour will be discussed in Chapter 4. Until parents begin to focus on the purposes of unsatisfactory behaviour, they will continue the ineffective approach of concentrating on the behaviour itself. We urge and coax children to eat, call them time and time again for meals, extol the virtues of learning and of completing homework, argue about television viewing, plead for less fighting and for more co-operation, constantly remind children to put their things away, and so it goes on. In so doing we simply play into children's hands and strengthen the unsatisfactory behaviours which our intervention was designed to weaken.

Consider children whom parents describe as 'lazy'. They need constant reminders to get up in the morning, to pack their school bag, to tidy their room, to put their toys away, or to take out the rubbish. Such children are on the receiving end of much parental criticism designed to make the child more responsible. The purpose of their behaviour is clear; it is to put parents into their service. Whose room do you tidy? Whose things do you put away? Whom do you have constantly to remind to finish chores? Lazy children will not learn from any form of criticism or punishment because their laziness achieves its purpose. Only when parents refuse to be put into the children's service and allow them to experience the consequences of their own behaviour will children begin to accept responsibility for those tasks which are legitimately theirs. Failure to identify the child's purpose results in a sequence of futile reactions which heighten parental feelings that they cannot manage, cope with, understand, or assist their children. Having tried all the various forms of correction, all to no avail, parents are left concluding: 'I just don't know what to do with George'.

It is important to recognise that emotions are created and generated to achieve a purpose. Children do not behave badly because they are emotionally upset but they become emotionally upset in order to misbehave. Emotions may be likened to the petrol in your car. Where does it take you? Nowhere. It needs a driver and the driver is the intellect which creates the emotion. As such, emotions are secondary to the intellect and are controlled by it. There are no faulty emotions but only faulty decisions as emotions are always viewed in terms of the purpose to be achieved.

Consider a young child who believes: 'I belong only if I can keep people busy with me.' Shyness is an appropriate emotion to generate as people indicate their willingness to give special service to the shy child. If people did not respond to the shyness, the child would no longer be shy as no purpose or goal is achieved by it. Crying is an attempt to regain control. Recently the author was counselling a woman who was divorced and had custody of a ten-year-old daughter. When the mother was advised to discontinue sleeping with the child and helping the child with homework each night, the child began to weep profusely. What is the child saying through her tears? 'Stop telling my mother those things. I will control her the way I want.' Tears are an attempt to regain control and should be viewed as gold-mines for further probing. Depression is a silent temper tantrum; apathy is a form of passive power; anger is an attempt to

control; sadness is designed to gain pity and try to secure a more effective situation, while guilt is an attempt to prove good intentions without a commitment to change.

Emotions are not the driving force behind behaviour but are the means individuals use to achieve a goal. If parents react to emotions at their surface level they will fail to see what is achieved by the various emotions. Once parents recognise how thought influences feeling which in turn generates action, they will be in a position to influence their children. How will you respond when your 5-year-old child comes home tomorrow and says: 'I had lunch all by myself at school today. Nobody wants to sit with me.' Hopefully along these lines: 'I am sorry that you didn't have a friend today but I am sure you will soon.' When the child's attempts to special service fail, there will be no point in trying to upset the parent.

It is a sad commentary on child rearing that the most common method used by parents to change a child's unacceptable behaviour is to resort to external pressure in the form of threats, criticism, force, punishment, or deprivation. Dawdling, swearing, lying, bad habits, disobedience, teasing, bad manners, stealing, and such are usually followed by punishment. The effectiveness of punishment, physical, emotional, or verbal, can be judged by the frequency with which parents punish the same behaviour. A mother recently reported that she had to intervene on a daily basis to stop the fighting between her 11-year-old and 13-year-old children. She had done that since the children were young — approximately 35 000 times! If it is the child's purpose to gain attention, then unacceptable behaviours are perfectly logical, rational, and sensible from the child's view and are, in fact, the best ways of behaving. To punish such behaviours is to do exactly what children want you to do and strengthens their belief that they belong when they disturb. Even the most antisocial behaviour is an expression by children of their means of finding a place in the family and is based on a mistaken or faulty idea that they cannot belong through constructive or acceptable means.

Each Child Has a Unique Pattern of Behaviour

We all have our own particular way of behaving which distinguishes us from one another. We have a particular view of ourselves and of our relationship to the environmenf. This typical way of behaving may be referred to as 'personality' or, as Adler described it, 'style of life'. It is the guiding theme in one's life and gives unity and stability to behaviour. To understand children we must be aware of their life style; to assist in their development we must understand the factors which contribute to the formation of life style.

Adler (1930:23) described the unity and pervasiveness of a child's life style when he wrote:

> The psychic life of a child is a wonderful thing and it fascinates at every point where one touches it. Perhaps the most remarkable fact of all is the way in which we must unroll the whole scroll of the child's life in order to understand a single event. Every act seems to express the whole of a child's life and personality and is thus unintelligible without a knowledge of this invisible background. To this phenomenon we give the name, unity of personality.

The formation of life style begins at birth as infants seek to understand their world and their relationship to it. As mentioned earlier, the young child operates on a trial-and-error basis and evaluates each activity in terms of its consequences. In evaluating these experiences, a child looks for guiding principles which will govern characteristic movements through life and will result in the establishment of a specific style of life. Once formed, a child's response to each new situation is decided by the particular life style which the child has adopted.

Consequently, the way in which a child views an event is more important than the event itself. 'The child's opinion of life is his own masterpiece.' The child who interprets the arrival of a new-born baby as a personal rejection and displacement is more likely to be influenced by this faulty interpretation than by the reality of the situation (Dreikurs, 1971:57):

> Our interpretation of the early experiences to which we are exposed distinguish us from any other human being. These early impressions form the basis of our self-concept, of our life style.

And again (Ausbacher, 1970:44):

> The individual is not blindly pushed by instinctual forces but pulled by his own ideas of success, which, in the last analysis, are actually his own creation. For man is free: he must accept his heredity and his environment, but the way he responds to these is determined subjectively and internally.

Life style is the result of a child's interpretation of his environment during the early years of life. It is not the particular experiences which the child has but rather the conclusions drawn from those experiences which determine life style. By the time children are five or six years old, they begin to integrate their subjective impressions of family living into typical ways of behaving, their life style, a plan of living which recurs throughout life as does a melody in a piece of music. From now on, children will perceive each situation not as it actually is, but as they wish to view it in terms of a particular life style.

Dreikurs (1954:9) has observed that:

> It is impossible to understand any adult without information about his first four to six years of life, which are the formative years. In this period, every person develops concepts about himself and about life which are maintained throughout life, although the person remains completely unaware of the premises he has developed for himself and upon which he acts.

For this reason, parent education is most important for it is the first five or six years of life which are critical in influencing an individual's view of self, life, and others. Rarely has the author dealt with a difficult adolescent who does not report a series of discouraging experiences early in the home life. Indeed, the test of parenting effectiveness comes in adolescence.

Having formulated a life style, children no longer grope on the basis of trial and error but act in accordance with a set of stable concepts. They view each event from their own personal bias or prejudice and their interpretation of experience is always in accord with the direction established by their life style. They adjust their perception to their own private logic and this enables them to act logically even though others may see their behaviour quite differently.

By the time children are ready to begin school, their life style has become fairly stable and their attitude to their environment will colour each new experience. School is not a totally novel experience for children as they will impose on their teachers and peers the way in which they want to be treated. A brother with a very clever sister may choose to be viewed as stupid; nothing will be expected of him and he will not be blamed for his mistakes. A girl who is physically small learns very early to use her size to her advantage. She observes that people are willing to do physical things for her such as carrying, lifting, and helping. She cultivates this advantage and at school will quickly have the teacher and her classmates feeling that she is in need of help and assistance, a service which they eagerly provide. 'You boys help Anne move her chair.' 'Let me do that for you Anne.' This pattern of behaviour, developed in the early years and reflected in the life style as: 'I know I belong as long as you will do things for me', will extend to the school, to the work situation, and into her adult life where she always seems able to induce people to render her special assistance.

In our society, certain life styles are common. Among those which may be identified are:

I have a place if I am taken care of by others.
I have a place if I am the most powerful one.
I have a place if I am in control.
I have a place if I am the smartest one.
I have a place if I am the funniest one.
I have a place if I am the most hopeless one.
I have a place if I am No. 1.

Think of the children you know who fit the above life styles — the clown, the bully, the scholar, the shy child, the cute child, the hopeless child, and the stubborn child. All are typical ways of belonging which come from faulty interpretations of early childhood experiences, and they will persist because children will initiate those experiences which they desire or anticipate and will exclude experiences which would be inconsistent with their life styles.

The problem is this. Some people believe that they belong *only if* they can be the best, the most powerful and so on. There is no flexibility in their lives so that their inability to satisfy the *only if* concept will result in their living miserable lives. We must communicate to children that they belong unconditionally and not only by being better, smarter and so on.

While the means of achieving the goals consistent with life style will vary with age, the goals themselves will not. For example, a girl whose life style is: 'I know that I belong when I am the best' may be the best student in primary school but find that she cannot be the best at secondary school. Instead of trying to be the best scholar, she may turn to being the best at organising, or being funny, or being the best athlete, or the best troublemaker or perhaps the most hopeless student. Although these behaviours differ widely, the goal behind them is the same: 'I know that I belong when I am the best.'

Why does a child's typical way of behaving remain stable after the age of five or six? It is because children do not see reality as it is but only as they need to see it. As beauty is in the eye of the beholder, so too is the world a product of a person's perception of it. 'The individual', wrote Adler, 'sees all his problems from a perspective which is his own creation.' While children are excellent observers, they do not always draw correct conclusions because they do not possess all of the facts. For example, a boy may see his parents' delight with the reading skill of his five-year-old sister and conclude that he can never read as well as she can. Another boy sees the additional responsibility and privileges given to his older sister and concludes that he has been unfairly treated. A girl with a long illness may incorrectly conclude that people are there to serve her, while a boy who is spoiled may think that he is entitled to receive everything he desires.

From these faulty conclusions emerge faulty life styles. Therefore, inappropriate behaviour is not regarded by the child as such because it is consistent with his life style. Adler (1930: 61–2) gives a good example. A boy at school, the laziest in the class, was asked by his teacher, 'Why do you get on so badly with your work?' He answered, 'If I am the laziest boy here, you will always be occupied with me. You never pay any attention to the good boys, who never disturb the class and do their work properly.' So long as it was his aim to attract notice and rule over his teacher, he had found the best way to do it. Thus, all of a child's actions and attitudes are expressions of life style and, to understand any particular behaviour, we need to study the total child, to look below the surface for the guiding influence on a child's behaviour, a child's life style.

What are the factors influencing a child's development? Traditional psychology, under the influence of Freud and neo-Freudians, would look to a series of critical phases in the early life of a child, particularly those involving the mother, such as feeding, weaning, and toilet training, and would consider parental practices and attitudes in relation to these problems as decisive influences on a child's personality.

Individual Psychology believes that the most important factor influencing life style is the child's ordinal position, the birth order within a family. Personality and character traits are expressive of movement within the family. They indicate the means by which children attempt to find their place within the family. Dreikurs is of the belief that the only fundamental law governing the development of a child's character is that 'he trains those qualities by which he hopes to achieve significance or even a degree of power and superiority in the family constellation'. (Dreikurs, 1950:41) Adler (1927:147) agrees and notes:

> Before we can judge a human being we must know the situation in which he grew up. An important moment is the position which a child occupied in his family constellation.*

* Family constellation is the relation of each member of the family to the others. Just as stars form a constellation, so does each family have its own constellation.

Importance of the Family Constellation

Children do not grow up in isolation but as a part of a family group. The family includes not only the parent or parents but other siblings, and it is the latter which exert the greatest influence on a child. Children in the same family each have a different environment because of their ordinal position. The second child is born into a different psychological situation from the first, and subsequent children all have a unique situation. It is not the actual birth order which is important but rather the psychological interpretation of the position. If the eldest child is unassertive, withdrawn, and lacking ambition, characteristics usually not found in the first, it is likely that the second child will be assertive, outgoing and ambitious. Birth order is not a determinant of behaviour but is a major influence on the types of behaviour which children adopt.

First-born Children

In the life style of every child there is the imprint of his or her position in the family. The first-born child is in the unique position of being, for a year or two, the only child. During that time the child is the sole object of the parents' attention, suffers from parental inexperience, and is subjected to more pressure, closer scrutiny, and higher expectations than any other member of the family. The position does have some rewards as the child establishes a 'kingdom' with a range of persons serving him — mother, father, uncles, aunts, and grandparents.

This rather attractive situation is rudely shattered by the arrival of the second child, an event for which the first cannot be adequately prepared. Clearly he is 'dethroned' and will strive to regain his 'rightful' place. Depending partly on the age gap and sex of the other child, the first-born is likely to conclude that he belongs only when he is the first or the best. From then on, there will be no mistakes in his behaviour, no doubts or uncertainties. The first-born will engage only in those activities where he can be the first or the best. He will enter school and attempt to be the best student. If he is unable to be the best at schoolwork, he may be the nicest child, the teacher's pet. Failing this, he can be the most powerful or vicious child in the class, the bully. And so he goes on, engaging in those activities only where he sees an opportunity of being the best. Frequently ambitious, first-born children are high achievers, more conservative, and fond of authority. It is not difficult to see why.

Second-born Children

The second-born child will almost invariably be what the first child is not. As the second child searches for behaviours which will provide her with a place within the family, she will become aware that there is someone ahead of her who is older, larger, and more capable and has already successfully staked his claim in certain areas. Whatever those areas are, the second will be careful to avoid them, as there is no point in competing with a more able person when there are so many other avenues available which will achieve the same purpose of belonging.

The second-born resembles a racehorse in the way she keeps on galloping forward in an attempt to overtake the first child. Her vision is directed to the future. The second child will frequently adopt behavioural patterns diametrically opposite to the first child. An indication of their extreme difference can be judged by the often repeated remark made by parents concerning their second child: 'Helen is just so different from John. I swear that we brought the wrong child home from hospital.' Extreme differences in personality are usually found between the first two children. Scholarly-unscholarly; quiet-noisy; co-operative-unco-operative; sport-non-sport; tidy-untidy; good eater-poor eater. Where one succeeds, the other gives up. Feeling unfairly treated because she does not have the privileges of the first, squeezed out by the arrival of a third child, the second has the most uncomfortable position in the family and will generally be the most difficult child for parents.

Competition is common between the first and second child as the second seeks to overtake and supplant the pacemaker in terms of parental attention. The oldest, believing that he belongs only when he is the best, acts to prevent the younger from competing success-fully in areas where the first is achieving well. For instance, when the second child brings her painting home from kindergarten, the following conversation is quite typical:

Younger child: Do you like my painting?

Mother: Yes dear, it's lovely.

Older child: She hasn't used many colours; she hasn't filled up the page.

What he is actually saying is, 'It is not as good as I can do and don't you ever forget it.'

Last-born Children

Youngest children quickly learn that they are surrounded by more able people, people who are prepared to do things for them, to make decisions for them, and to take responsibility for them. As a result they may decide to retain this baby role and place people in their service.

Being last-born has its advantages. You are never displaced by other children and have parents who are generally better established economically. Further, the last born has fewer parental pressures placed upon him and does not suffer from parental inexperience. Look at the baby book for the first-born 'where every step, every landmark, every tooth, every stage of development is lovingly recorded, often documented with pictures and drawings'. (Dreikurs and Grey, 1970:11) The last child is lucky if his name is even recorded in the book. Photographs abound of the first child but are virtually non-existent for the youngest. Pressure is off last-born children, as more experienced and older parents do not demonstrate their fierce concern for their development and are more inclined to let the children be themselves. While these children tend to have a problem in developing independence, of breaking away from their baby image, they benefit by frequently having relaxed and pleasing personalities.

Only Children

Only children have a difficult position as the advantage gained in having no other child to displace them is more than offset by the fact that they live much of their life in an adult world and their childhood is spent with people who are always more proficient. Their orientation is to adults and their choice is to join them or to be served by them. Depending on the particular decision made, only children will tend to become precocious or 'hopelessly baby', behaviours which will not gain them acceptance by peers. It is important that the only child be brought into contact with other children at an early age through play groups, pre-school, and home visits by other children. This will help them develop the social skills of relating to other children, skills which will not be acquired in the adult world.

While the effect of a child's ordinal position in the family is naturally influenced by the size of the family, the ages and sex of the children, and parental reaction to children and to each other, parents are urged to consider the effects which children have on each other and how often these effects reflect ordinal position. Children use their position in the family to develop particular character traits. Competition between children is always expressed through differences in temperament, interests, and abilities.

> As each member strives for his own place within the group, the competing opponents watch each other carefully to see the ways and means by which the opponent succeeds or fails. Where one succeeds, the other gives up; where one shows weakness or deficiencies, the other steps in. (Pepper, n.d.)

It is, however, the parents' reaction to children's behaviours which is critical rather than the ordinal position. Change this reaction and children's behaviour will change.

Loss of Confidence Leads to Misbehaviour

In their efforts to find a place in the family, children meet with many difficulties. Their initial attempts at achieving, contributing, and co-operating are often discouraged by parents, and children begin to lose faith in their ability to cope with the demands of the situation. A three-year-old boy who offers to clear the dishes from the table, help unpack the messages, or run an errand will frequently find that his offers are refused by parents on the grounds of: 'too small', 'too heavy', 'too slow'. When a young girl attempted to remove the eggs from their carton, she was told: 'Oh, no dear, you are too small and might break them.' What the child is being told in this and similar incidents is: 'As you are now, you are not much good. When you are older, stronger, bigger, faster, and smarter, that's when you will be all right.'

Children know that they are smaller, less competent, and less powerful than adults, but it is the interpretation of their experiences of these factors when compared with other adults and siblings which is so important. When their early attempts at contributing to the home routine are rejected on the above grounds, children begin to feel that they are not good enough and that they cannot belong to the family through useful behaviours. Consequently their development of social interest is inhibited, and feelings of inferiority begin to make their appearance in the form of unsatisfactory and unacceptable behaviour.

Too often we impress children with our own efficiency, strength, speed, size, and ability. A boy might struggle for ten minutes to tie his laces, a task which an impatient mother does for him in three seconds. A poorly made bed which required considerable time and effort by a child is 'corrected' by father in seconds. Children lacking feeding skills will find the task removed from them; a poor dresser will be dressed by a parent. We take over the responsibilities of our children and impress them with their inadequacies. We refuse to accept children as they are but conditionally on being better. The promise of the future — 'later on', 'bigger', 'older', and 'stronger' — is a universal source of discouragement to children.

The home is a learning environment in which children must acquire a large number of skills. Many of these are taught incidentally and inadequately. Even among those parents who do attempt to carefully transmit skills, there are many who refuse to accept a child's current level of performance as they feel that such acceptance will prevent the child from improving. From the child's viewpoint, nothing is ever good enough because it could always be better. As a consequence, many children are poorly prepared to meet their increasing responsibilities for dressing, eating, toilet training, personal care, playing, speaking and relating to other children. They have become discouraged through their home experiences which have impressed them with their inadequacy, deficiency, and imperfection.

Two other factors contribute to these feelings of inferiority. Firstly, other children who are already more proficient in performing the various skills are used as standards of comparison. A child is reminded that whatever he is doing has been done or is being done more proficiently by a sister or brother. 'Why don't you keep your room tidy like Sally?' 'Why don't you read clearly like Jim?' 'Jane could dress herself when she was your age.' 'Why don't you get good marks like Sandra?' The child concludes: 'Give up, I can never be as good as others.'

A second source of discouragement is the mistaken methods of child rearing which result in the child being deprived of opportunities to experience his or her own strengths and abilities. Harmful approaches include spoiling, pampering, rejection, neglect, overprotection, indulgence, nagging, fault-finding, excessive talking, lovelessness, and physical punishment. In various ways, these approaches deny children the opportunity of learning that they are wanted and respected members of the family and are able to make a useful contribution to the family.

In a competitive society many parents want to be 'super' parents. They want their children to have a happy childhood and they give them everything. Children develop ideas that they belong only if

they are the centre of the family and that they immediately get whatever they want. This is not a happy, constructive human being because the real solution to life is in giving, working for others, contributing to the group and co-operating. Spoiled children, when they are outside the pampered circle, feel themselves constantly threatened and act as though they are in a hostile country.

From these various sources of discouragement, children develop a sense of inferiority which impels them to strive on the 'useless'* side of life. Fearing defeat on the useful side of life, children's basic urge to participate, to meet problems and difficulties of life as they come along, is sidetracked and their goal now becomes one of self-centredness, self-enhancement, and personality superiority over others.

> All maladjustment is characterised by an underdeveloped social interest. The life goal of the maladjusted is personal superiority and power over others . . . Self centredness is not the normal condition of man but a sign of maladjustment. (Ansbacher, 1970:44)

All misbehaviour in children is due to a loss of self-confidence, to a sense of inferiority resulting from discouragement. Human failure is not the cause of inferiority but is the consequence of such feeling. Our ineffective parenting techniques, our refusal to accept children as they are, our comparison of child with child, and our constant

---

* 'Useless' side of life refers to behaviours which demonstrate no interest in or concern for others, which reveal a lack of co-operation, and which are directed towards personal superiority and power over others.

concern with correcting inadequate behaviour leads many children to give up in despair. Instead of facing the problems of friendship, school, occupation, and sexual matters with confidence, they turn to unacceptable behaviours in their belief that this will gain them a sense of importance and belonging.

If parents would set out to provide each child with a set of encouraging experiences, to refrain from criticism, to use approaches which communicate respect, to focus on a child's abilities rather than his or her disabilities, they would greatly assist children in their personal development and would lay the foundations for the development of a healthy personality.

Try these

(1) Which parent creates a feeling of inferiority in John who has received a B grade in mathematics?

    A John, I know you can do better than this. You received an A last time.

    B John, I see from your report that you like mathematics. It's good fun isn't it?

                                    (A)

(2) Describe the behaviours which are likely of Sally, a six-year-old whose older brother Richard, seven years, is described as being:

| noisy | untidy | lazy |
| forgetful | unpunctual | mathematically able |

                                    (   )

(3) You have great difficulty in getting Robert, aged eight, off to bed. He has to be told three or four times and often needs to be smacked before he goes. What is his likely life style?

    A I know I belong when I am the most powerful one.

    B I know I belong when I am taken care of by others.

                                    (A)

(4) Which mother knows about the purpose of behaviour?

    A 'Kate won't put anything away. She is so lazy.'

    B 'Kate is lazy so that she has me putting her things away.'

                                  (B)

(5) Which principle is the father violating when he says to his eight-year-old son: 'Tim, you know that it is wrong to take money from the housekeeping purse?'

A The basic motivation is to belong.
B Deal with behaviour in the total group.
C Life style is patterned and unified.

(6)

Answers

(1) Parent (A) discourages because John is told that his work is not good enough because it could be better. While that may be true, it is not the way to encourage John to do better. John feels that he is no good because he did not do as well as his parents desired.

(2) Sally will probably be very different from Richard: quiet, reliable, tidy, responsible, punctual, and not good at mathematics. Why is she likely to demonstrate these characteristics? Because she finds her place more easily by being what Richard is not. It is not inevitable but it is highly likely, particularly in a competitive family.

(3) Style (A). He can prove his importance by being the most powerful one. He fights and continues to fight.

(4) Mother (B). She knows that the purpose of Kate's behaviour is to put mother into her service. Mother (A) concentrates on a description of the behaviour, i.e. 'lazy' but fails to go the one step further to identify the purpose of being lazy.

(5) Principle (B). Always deal with unsatisfactory behaviour by involving the total family. Members of the family influence the behaviour of each other and they must assist in any corrective program. If the child steals to get even because he feels that he is disliked by other members of the family, who should try to convince the child that he is liked, the father or the members of the family?

3
The Purposes of Children's Misbehaviour

Introduction

The previous chapter emphasised a number of basic principles which may be used as a guide to understanding children's behaviour. One of these principles indicated that children are purposeful in their behaviour, that in their striving to belong, they direct their activities towards clearly defined goals. Consequently, behaviour can be understood only by examining or observing its consequences, that is, goals, the results which the behaviour achieves rather than the behaviour itself. Adler (1957:29) stated this view when he wrote:

> The psychic life of man is determined by his goal. No human being can think, feel, will, dream, without all these activities being determined, continued, modified, and directed towards an ever present objective.

We have previously considered the influences which affect a child during the time when life style is being formed. The family constellation, methods of training, and the family atmosphere created by parents will interact to produce a unique life style in each child. The life style then provides a behavioural theme for a child's future dealings with parents, siblings, teachers, and others in his or her environment. Because their interpretation of early experiences is often faulty, children frequently develop inappropriate life styles. They feel that they are not able to belong by constructive means and, instead, turn to inappropriate goals in their attempt to find a place and to gain status.

Individuals are not influenced by what they are or how they developed that way, but by what they aim to achieve, their intention or their goal. Of the three influences, the past, the present and the future, only the latter can be changed. Individuals are not driven through life by the past but impelled to go forward into the future.

The major influence on behaviour is not the push of the past but the pull of the future.

It is only when one understands the nature of children's goals that one understands children. There is little to be gained in attempting to determine *how* a child developed in a particular way, for example, spoilt or rejected; or *what* a child is at present, for example, lazy, selfish, or anxious; or to look for deficiencies or disabilities in a child. Children cannot change what they are or how they got that way; that is in the past. However, they can change the purposes of their behaviour because they are in the future. From a child's point of view, it is extraordinarily refreshing to have somebody talk to them about the purposes of their behaviour. They think: 'Here at last is somebody who understands me.' Children are not aware of the purposes of their actions and are therefore unable to change their behaviour. 'Bad' children would prefer to be 'good' but do not know how to stop being 'bad'. Make them aware of the goal behind their disturbing behaviour and they can change their behaviour.

The inability to change children's behaviour without a knowledge of their goals is evidenced by the many thousands of children whose reading levels are deplorably low. How do the 'experts' explain this problem? They blame the parents, the broken home, progressive or open education, teachers, or the children themselves. Look at the variety of reasons which are offered to explain a child's poor reading. The child is disadvantaged, deprived, has cultural or perceptual deprivation, is autistic, dyslexic, suffers from disorders of the central nervous system, has problems of visual and auditory modalities, has brain damage, is handicapped by intrasensory or intersensory disabilities, special visual distortion, aphasias, disgraphias, incomplete cerebral dominance, sidedness, and so on. One interesting explanation which was recently offered described the child as a 'perceptual cripple'. A hundred and one excuses are necessary to explain poor reading only because teachers do not understand the purposes of a child's lack of progress. Learning progress does not depend on a child's abilities or disabilities but is always a reflection of the decisions which a child has made. In many cases, children choose not to learn to read because they can involve people with them by not reading. Teachers, parents, remedial teachers, psychologists, and psychiatrists all become involved with a seven-year-old girl who decides not to read. We must tackle the decision rather than the behaviour because the behaviour is an expression of the child's purpose, her decision.

Stand back and observe your daughter when she misbehaves. Ask yourself, 'What does the child achieve in behaving this way? To whom is the behaviour directed? What do I do when she misbehaves? What is her response to my correction?' This line of thinking will help you to become aware of children's purposes and you will see the logic of the child's behaviour. What was previously incomprehensible, illogical, and foolish behaviour will become very meaningful.

One of our greatest mistakes is to concentrate on the behaviour itself rather than look for the purpose of the behaviour. Children who lie, steal, become sullen, disobedient, moody, or stubborn receive a talking to about the dire consequences of these behaviours, are punished and advised to mend their ways. Frequent and careful explanations are given as to the undesirability of such behaviours, particularly those relating to stealing, lying, and moral issues. Do you think that children do not know that they should not lie and steal? The parents are behaving exactly as the children wish and this is why they will continue to lie and steal. By cautioning, rebuking, punishing, and suppressing, parents are doing what children would want them to. The inappropriate ways of behaving will continue because they are effective in achieving a purpose.

In their relationships with children, parents should view behaviour in terms of its goals. Only then will they make an appropriate response. Ask not 'whence' but 'whither'. A child who feels that his importance lies in being the most powerful member of the family will pursue those behaviours which provide opportunities for challenge. He will be defiant, disobedient, argumentative, stubborn, and unco-operative. Nobody can make him do anything. Such a child, believing that his position depends on refusing to do what the parents want, looks for opportunities to defeat them. If parents understood the purpose behind these forms of misconduct, refused to fight with the child, openly admitted that they cannot make him do anything, there would be little point in the child continuing to behave in these ways. It takes two to fight and a child who cannot involve a parent in a power contest has lost. Behaviours such as disobedience, defiance and stubbornness, being no longer effective, are likely to change.

What Are the Goals of Misbehaviour?

All disturbing behaviour of children is directed towards one of four possible goals. Children may attempt through their behaviour to:

(1) gain attention;
(2) demonstrate power;
(3) seek revenge;
(4) escape by withdrawal.

Because these goals are not apparent, parents constantly strengthen unacceptable behaviour by reacting to it. We cannot begin to help our children until we are aware of the meaning of their behaviour, can identify the goals of misbehaviour, and respond appropriately.

The four goals and examples of the behaviours which reflect the goals are presented in Figure 1. Behaviours in each goal may be 'attacking', where the child is actively pursuing a goal; or 'defending', in which case the child passively achieves the desired result. For instance, a child whose goal is power may contradict you frequently or may refuse to do what he is told; the former attacks in his pursuit of power while the latter defends.

Attention Seeking

Attention seeking is by far the most common form of misbehaviour found in young children. The reason for its high frequency may be found in the way in which children are raised. In the first five or six years of life during which children are attempting to develop a life style, what opportunities do we provide for them to participate usefully and functionally within the family? What tasks do the children perform which enable them to conclude that they belong because of their ability to contribute to the family? Go back to a previous generation when there were fewer labour-saving devices. Children had particular jobs to perform such as setting the fire, cutting wood, feeding fowls, collecting eggs, and the like. Children knew they belonged because they contributed. With all the labour-saving devices available, the situation is totally different. Mostly we do not assign any responsibilities to young children and, therefore, deny them the opportunity of concluding that they are useful members of the family and able to participate in its functioning. How then, does the young child gain a sense of belonging?

The child is forced to rely upon others, particularly the parent. A four-year-old who greets her father each evening with 'Have you brought me something home Daddy?' is really saying, 'As long as you keep bringing me things home I know I belong.' A child who makes incessant demands on the mother is saying, 'Unless I can keep

CHILD'S GOAL: TYPES OF MISBEHAVIOUR

	Attacking behaviour	Defending behaviour
Attention seeking	The 'nuisance' The 'clown' The 'smart alec' The 'walking question-mark' Mischief-maker Embarrassment of people Unpredictable actions Obtrusiveness Instability	Bashfulness or shyness Fearfulness Anxiety Tearfulness Wanting help Eating problems Laziness Self-indulgence Untidiness
Power	Rebellion Argumentativeness Defiance Contradicting Disobedience (carrying out forbidden acts) Temper tantrums Bullying 'Bossiness' 'Bad Habits'	Stubbornness Lack of co-operation Dawdling Forgetfulness Disobedience (refusal to do what he's told)
Revenge	Stealing Viciousness Destructiveness Cruelty 'Tough Guy' Violence Brutality Delinquent behaviour Bed wetting	Sullenness Moodiness Moroseness Refusal to participate Passive hatred
Escape by withdrawal		'Hopelessness' Stupidity Idleness Incapability Inferiority complex Babyish ways Fantasy activities Solitary activities Refusal to mix

Figure 1   Classification of Behaviour with Undesirable Goals

you busy with me, I am nothing.' Lacking opportunities to belong usefully, children gain a sense of belonging by keeping parents involved with them. All attention-seeking behaviour of children, be it attacking or defending, is designed to put adults into their service. The range of these behaviours is remarkably wide, as seen by the examples presented in Figure 2.

CHILD'S GOAL: ATTENTION SEEKING

Attacking behaviour		Defending behaviour	
Child's strategy	Parent's reaction	Child's strategy	Parent's reaction

Being a nuisance
The 'show-off'
The 'clown'
The 'smart alec'
The 'walking
   question mark'
Pushing,
   obtrusiveness
Making mischief
Embarrassing
   behaviour
'You never know
   what he'll do
   next'
'Model' child
Instability
	Annoyance and
	   irritation
	'For goodness sake,
	   stop it.'
	Feeling of relief
	   when annoying
	   behaviour ceases
		Laziness
		Bashfulness;
		   shyness
		Fearfulness
		Anxiety
		Tearfulness
		Wanting help
		'Tiredness'
		Untidiness
		Eating problems
		Self-indulgence
		Vanity
		Cuteness
			'I must do
			   something.'
			Urging or coaxing
			   into action
			Feeling of
			   encouragement
			   when child
			   responds

Figure 2   Types of Behaviour Classified as Attention Seeking and Parental Reactions to Them

Attention Seeking: Attacking Behaviour

One form of attention-seeking behaviour is that in which a child actively provokes or attacks in a way that parents cannot ignore. While these behaviours may annoy and irritate parents, they are very effective in achieving their purpose. You certainly know that the child is around when he chooses these ways of behaving.

Many of these behaviours classified as 'attacking' are frequently viewed favourably by parents. Examples of such behaviours are bright sayings, exaggerated conscientiousness, clowning, persistent questioning, or being the 'model' child. In assessing the nature of problem behaviour, we have viewed misbehaving children as discouraged children who feel that, as they are, they are not good enough and who react to the feeling of inferiority by striving for goals which have a purely personal or private meaning. No longer is the child interested in co-operating with others to meet the demands of each situation, but only with self-enhancement, self-elevation, and a desire to be better than others. All misbehaviour in children is their mistaken belief that this will take them above other children.

To differentiate between behaviour which has attention seeking as its goal, and behaviour which stems from a genuine desire to contribute and co-operate, a parent should ask the question, 'Would this behaviour continue if I were to ignore it?' Attention-seeking behaviour will cease because it no longer works. There is no point in showing off if nobody responds; clowning is purposeless without an audience who laughs. A 'model' child who is a model for the purpose of gaining attention will cease to be a model child if the behaviours are not constantly praised. What the child seeks through model behaviour is your constant approval, the receipt of which elevates the child above others in the family. 'Why can't you keep your room as tidy as Karen's?' 'Why don't you do your school work as well as Jane?' While model behaviour is not a short-term problem to the parent, time will be the enemy of such children as they must later enter more competitive situations where they cannot shine or excel. In these cases, such children simply give up because they cannot be the best.

How effective are these attention-seeking behaviours? Just think of the number of times you stop to rebuke, correct, prevent, remind, punish, or admonish your children and you will realise how efficient children are in achieving their goals. The strange part is that parents are totally unaware of the game being played. They fail to see that almost all of the annoying and irritating behaviour of children is for the parent's benefit. Simply, the child misbehaves in order to gain your attention. See such behaviours for what they are. Stand back and observe how skilfully children are able to involve and control you almost all day long. When you consider the purpose behind attacking behaviours, you will see that you are the unwitting target of children's mistaken belief that they belong only as long as they can keep you busy with them. They act in such a way as to say: 'Stop whatever you are doing and pay attention to me. I belong only as long as I can attract your attention'.

Attention Seeking: Defending Behaviour

In contrast to the child who actively intrudes or disturbs for the purpose of gaining attention, is the one who achieves a similar goal by remaining passive, by not doing things, or by defending or retreating from situations. Such children gain a feeling of belonging by placing parents in their service through general passivity.

If parents were asked to list those behaviours which worry them most in their children, those belonging to the defending attention-seeking category would not appear frequently. Behaviours such as vanity, cuteness, charmer and 'clinging vine' are often admired by parents because the children who display them are usually very pleasant and are favourites with both teachers and parents alike. The fact that these children are completely dependent on others, initiate nothing themselves, and doubt their ability to contribute usefully in group situations goes unnoticed. They defend against the reality of inadequacy by inviting others to accept their responsibilities.

Parents should ask themselves the reason for a child's dependence on them. Would children be so charming and pleasant if they did not receive special recognition? Is their lack of initiative a result of concluding that they receive the most attention when parents view them as needing special service or assistance? Such children are more discouraged than those who engage in attacking behaviour but, unfortunately, many will remain discouraged because nobody bothers to redirect them. They are frequently just too pleasant.

Vanity is a common form of defending behaviour. How does a child become vain? Diana was a particularly attractive child who frequently received favourable comments about her appearance from people with whom she came into contact. As a result, she began to expect such compliments. She noticed, however, that people did not comment on the things she was doing and concluded that what she was doing was not very good. On the basis of this recurring pattern of observations, Diana developed a life style which said that her belonging depended on her ability to attract comment for what she *was* rather than for what she *did*. At school, Diana gained frequent recognition from her teacher for her well-groomed and attractive features and was often sent on errands by the teacher. In time, Diana came to contribute less and less in terms of school achievement because she doubted her ability to do so. However, she began to demand more and more in terms of how she looked because she lived in dread of not being able to do so. How she will end up is problematical but it is no small coincidence that many physically attractive women seek the advice of psychiatrists when their physical beauty begins to deteriorate and that many physically attractive men buy fast sports cars and need to be seen in the company of young women when their handsomeness begins to fade. The message is clear: 'Never praise children for what they are but only what they do'. Attention seeking is an unrealistic goal which requires constant feeding. It is through contributing, rather than receiving, that a child can gain a real and lasting sense of belonging and worth. Probably the most important message which parents must teach their children is that you belong in this world by contributing rather than by taking.

There are other forms of defending behaviour which are more stressful to parents. Laziness, bashfulness, fearfulness, tearfulness, tiredness, self-indulgence, untidiness, and eating difficulties all have the effect of putting parents into the service of their children. In many homes, mothers are little short of being servants, doing a child's bidding, and performing chores which rightly belong to the child. A child who is slow in dressing, in tying shoe laces, in coming to the table, in tidying up, in completing homework, and in getting off to bed makes unfair demands upon a parent's time and energy. Children are slow in order to win special service. For a child whose life style is: 'I know I belong only when people are occupied with me', what better way of achieving this goal than by being slow, dependent, or lazy? Adler made the interesting observation that beauty is an organ inferiority. Do you see his point? How do attractive children use their attractiveness?

Consider the number of homes in which children are regarded as 'eating problems'. The number is so great that one is tempted to conclude that the universal hunger drive has been lost in this generation of children, a conclusion which many infant welfare sisters and parents would endorse. Why are there so many finnicky eaters? What purpose is achieved? Here is a typical family situation. Mother decides that Johnny is a little on the small side, frail, not as robust as others, underweight because of illness, or needing a more adequate diet. Subtle pressure is applied to the child: 'Come on

Johnny, just another mouthful.' When parents persist in encouraging a child to eat, the child rightly concludes that his eating behaviour is of more importance to them than it is to himself. Having reached this decision, Johnny is able to control his parents by refusing to eat whenever he wants attention. Mealtimes centre around him. His favourite dishes are prepared; he is constantly coaxed and urged to eat; meat is cut up for him; parents feed him at the table; and his half-hearted attempts at eating are generously praised.

In many homes, mealtimes are a tragic farce as parents battle to have children eat. Yet eating problems are avoidable and the solution to existing problems is simple once the goal is identified. A child's eating behaviour is not a topic of conversation. The parent's attitude should be this: 'If Johnny eats, it is because he is hungry. If he is not eating, it is because he is not hungry.' The first course is presented to all at the table. If Johnny chooses not to eat, nothing is said to him, for his eating is his own business. First-course dishes are then removed except for Johnny's, and the second course is served. As Johnny is demonstrably not hungry, he receives no second course. At the end of the meal, all dishes are removed including Johnny's uneaten first course. Johnny is given no food between meals and the same procedure is repeated at the next meal. If Johnny protests between meals about being hungry, he is pleasantly told: 'I am sorry that you are hungry but you know what to do about it.' What does Johnny learn? If he doesn't eat, he gets hungry. Who is distressed by his hunger? Nobody but himself; neither mother nor father has commented on his non-eating. Johnny will soon discover that it is more satisfying to eat regularly at mealtimes because there is nothing to be gained by eating poorly. In other words, when he discovers that the attention-seeking behaviour (his non-eating) is unsuccessful, it will be discontinued.

Never do for children what they can do for themselves. The author recently encountered a family where the mother hand-fed a 10-year-old because she wanted her to have 'one good meal'. Is the mother playing a responsible role? When children complain about the consequences which their inadequate behaviour has produced, be not impressed, remain firm and friendly, and reply: 'I am sorry that this has happened to you but you know what to do about it.' For example, a child who refuses to do her homework despite being reminded by a parent must experience the consequence of her behaviour in the classroom. When the child comes home from school that evening and complains of being punished for not having the work completed, a parent might respond with: 'I am sorry that you got into trouble but you know what to do about it.' We cannot teach children responsibility if we are going to shield them from irresponsibility. In this way, a parent avoids undue service such as reminding the child time after time to complete her homework. It is the child's responsibility to complete the work and she will experience the consequences at school.

Look always for the purpose behind inadequate behaviour and frequently you will find that it is an attempt to put you into a child's service. By recognising this purpose and refusing to comply, you can assist your children to develop more adequate and independent methods of coping with their problems and, at the same time, free yourself of the constant unreasonable demands which children make upon you.

Before leaving the area of attention-seeking behaviour, check that you are able to classify the following forms of misbehaviour.

Try these

Forms of attention seeking	Behaviour of child
A Attacking behaviours B Defending behaviours	1 Your child is very shy when introduced to people. ( )
	2 When you have visitors, your child interrupts with smart sayings. ( )
	3 Despite your frequent rebukes, your child embarrasses you when out in public. ( )
	4 Despite your reassurances, your young child cries whenever a dog approaches. ( )

Answers
1 (B); 2 (A); 3 (A); 4 (B)

Power

The struggle for power in our society has grown out of all proportion and parents are being drawn into contests with their children from which they cannot escape. Many homes are full of acts of retaliation as parents strive to maintain their traditional dominance and auth-

ority over children who, in turn, refuse to be dominated or suppressed. A state of 'open warfare' exists in some homes as both child and parent are locked into battle, each intent on scoring a 'victory' over the other. The need to understand behaviour which has power as its goal has never been greater.

Behaviours which demonstrate power are disobedience, temper tantrums, stubbornness, dawdling, masturbation, 'bad' habits, argumentativeness, defiance, untruthfulness, and bullying. As with attention seeking, power-goal behaviours may be either attacking or defending. Examples of the behaviours together with the parents' typical reaction or feeling about them are presented in Figure 3.

CHILD'S GOAL: POWER

Attacking behaviour		Defending behaviour	
Child's strategy	Parent's reaction	Child's strategy	Parent's reaction
Rebellion	Sense of being	Stubbornness	Exasperation
Arguing	provoked	Unco-operation	Irritation
Defiance	Anger	Dawdling	Sense of being
Truancy	Sense of authority	Forgetfulness	challenged
Contradicting	being challenged	Disobedience	'You won't get out
Disobedience	Desire to get on top	(won't do what	of it this way.'
(carries out	'If you think I'm	he is told)	'You'll fall into line,
forbidden acts)	going to stand for	Apathy	or else!'
Temper tantrums	this, you're	Frequent sickness	'Have it your own
Bullying	mistaken!'		way. See if I care.'
'Bossiness'	'I'll teach you to		Feeling of victory
'Bad habits'	defy me!'		when child falls
Thumb-sucking	'We'll see about		into line
Nail-biting	that!'		
Masturbation	Feeling of victory		
Teeth-grinding	when behaviour		
Head-rocking	is quelled		

Figure 3   Types of Behaviour Classified as Power and Parental Reactions to Them

Consider a boy who is difficult to get out of bed in the morning, is slow in dressing, refuses to tidy his room, comes home late from school, and will not go to bed at night without a display of force. What do these behaviours mean? Why do they upset parents? What the child is saying through these behaviours is this: 'I can prove my importance by refusing to do what you want.'; or 'I can prove my importance by doing whatever I like.' Children who hold a life style in which they feel they belong only by being the most powerful, are obliged to challenge you; to prove to you that you cannot make them do anything; to make themselves the most powerful member of the family. Whether this is through attacking behaviour ('You cannot stop me') or defending behaviour ('You cannot make me'), children are usually able to defeat you and strengthen their mistaken belief that they belong only by being the most powerful.

Children who engage in power struggles upset parents who feel that their authority is being challenged. We have a tradition of children doing what they are told. Today, telling a child what he or she must do is almost a certain way to provoke a fight. In the case of the boy already mentioned, what he is saying to you is: 'I will get up when I am ready to get up, I will go to bed when I am ready to go, and I will come home when I am ready to come home.' On the other hand, what the parent is actually saying is: 'You will get up when I tell you to get up, you will go to bed when I tell you to go, and you will come home from school when I tell you to come home.'

Without realising it, many parents have become more interested in maintaining control over children than in the welfare of their children. They may rationalise their demands that the child eats what they give him, or that he goes to bed when they tell him, on the grounds that they know best what a child needs in relation to food and rest. In reality, many are simply attempting to dominate their children with the unspoken demand: 'You will do what I tell you to do.' It is this autocratic demand which so many children resist today. It is the same demand which produced such violent reactions from labour, women, blacks, and students.

Regardless of the outcome of a power contest, a child has won whenever you let yourself be drawn into a battle. Power is important only when it is contested and a child who is unable to involve a parent in a struggle has lost. It takes two to fight and, if you will not fight, the child loses. There can be no victor in an empty field. For example, if a mother asks her daughter to pick up her toys from the floor and the child makes no attempt to do so, a wise parent will not ask a second time as this simply invites disobedience. Recognising that the purpose of the child's disobedience is to demonstrate power ('You can't make me do anything'), mother will say nothing more, pick up the toys herself if they are obstructing her movements or activities, and allow the child to experience the consequences of disorder. One such consequence is that, when mother puts things away, the child does not know where her toys are when she wants them next. The point is this: whenever you find yourself getting caught up in a power contest, your best approach is to leave the scene of the conflict and not become involved. By doing so, you defuse the situation, and in a sense 'win' because the child was not able to involve you in the power struggle. Remember, you cannot overpower a 'power-drunk' child.

On those occasions when parents do enter a power contest and make a child do their bidding such as picking up clothes, turning off the TV, taking out the rubbish bins or brushing teeth, what have the parents taught the child? Precisely this: power is important because the person with the power won. The child's mistaken belief about the importance of power is confirmed, so next time (and there will be a next time very soon) the child simply becomes more skilful in the way he or she uses power. Observe the child next time you have visitors. Victory for him is only a matter of time. His faulty life style, 'I belong only if I am the most powerful one', will be strengthened and behaviours such as disobedience and stubbornness will increase in frequency and intensity.

The use of power by children has become widespread in recent years. Conflict which has always existed in the past is now plainly visible as the dominance of parents over children has weakened with the advent of more democratic relationships. It is an interesting observation that matters over which parents and children fight are never the real issues. The game which children are playing is this: 'Who wins and who loses.' They are not concerned about the desirability of picking up toys or going to bed. Children engage in these behaviours to involve parents in a power struggle. 'I am not going to tell you again. Get in there and tidy up your room.' What game is the child playing with mother? 'Who wins and who loses.' 'Will mother get so sick of the room that she will tidy it up or will she make me do it?' Recognise that when you fight with a child, the content of the dispute is irrelevant — the issue is always the same, winning or losing.

Parents must stop fighting with their children if they are going to help them. One of the most important lessons which a parent must learn is to sidestep the struggle for power. Whenever you feel personally challenged or frustrated by a child's action or lack of action, withdraw from the situation. Do not be provoked into power contests but look for methods of dealing with the situation which take into account the needs of the situation rather than your own personal desire. These methods will be discussed in later chapters. Remember this: you cannot make a child do anything. We can invite cooperation, state what we intend to do, and encourage the child, but, in the final analysis, children are the only ones who can decide what they will do.

Try these

Forms of power goal	Behaviour of child
A Attacking behaviours B Defending behaviours	1 Joan continues to throw temper tantrums in the market when she doesn't get what she wants. ( )
	2 Jim has been told three times to pick up his coat. It still lies there. ( )
	3 'I wish you would stop contradicting everything I say.' ( )

	4	'Can't you ever remember to bring your smock home?'
		( )

Answers

1 (A); 2 (B); 3 (A); 4 (B)

Revenge

Some children feel that they are unfairly treated within a family and pursue a goal to seek revenge against parents, siblings, members of society, and society itself. These children may display attacking behaviours such as stealing, violence, brutality, destruction, cruelty, and forms of delinquency. Or, passively, the child may exhibit defending behaviours such as being sullen, morose, moody, and refusing to participate in family activities. The range of behaviours characterising revenge together with parental feelings and reactions are presented in Figure 4.

Children who have revenge as their goal are so discouraged that they have given up hope of belonging through constructive activities and now feel that the only way to gain recognition is to retaliate against those people and that society which denies them a place. They provoke hostility in order to be recognised. Dreikurs (1968:29) has described the revenge child: 'The mutual antagonism has become so strong that each party has only one desire: retaliation, to revenge his own feeling of being hurt.' By damaging public transport, burning down schools, lighting bush-fires, stealing cars, beating up older people, hurting their parents and siblings, revengeful children can at least gain some satisfaction in getting even and obtain some social position by being disliked. These children and young people see themselves as worthless, unfairly treated, pushed around, and disliked. They behave accordingly, attempt little else but revengeful behaviour, and generate in others considerable resentfulness, hostility, dislike, and a desire to punish — an unhappy cycle indeed.

The principal objective in helping children whose goal is revenge is to convince them that they can be liked and accepted, that there is a place for them in the group or the family. Yet everything they do tends to make us dislike them more. They are destructive, sullen, cruel or violent; they know how to hurt and they do it often. When

their offences are detected, they are punished and told what des-
picable people they are. A child who deliberately inflicts a painful
burn on his younger sister will be severely punished and told what
a horrible child he is. An adolescent who rips the train seats will also
be punished and reminded that he is a nasty vicious lout. The effect
of punishment will be to cause the individual to retaliate and seek
further revenge. The result of being told that one is vicious, contemptible, worthless, and the like is to confirm the faulty evaluation
which the individual already holds. He will continue to behave in a
manner expected of a contemptible person. The circle is now complete, a self-fulfilling prophecy. We communicate to a child that he
is disliked, nasty, or vicious and he behaves accordingly. These children are fighting with society and are willing to 'accept the fortunes
of war'. (Dreikurs and Grey, 1968:39)

While parents display a marked inability to cope with the revengeful child, our schools fare much worse. Repeatedly we hear of children being expelled from school for various acts of vandalism, dis-

CHILD'S GOAL: REVENGE

Attacking behaviour		Defending behaviour	
Child's strategy	Parent's reaction	Child's strategy	Parent's reaction
Viciousness	Feeling of being	Sullenness	Feeling of injustice
'Tough guy'	badly upset; a	Moodiness	Feeling of being 'got
Violence	little fear	Moroseness	at'
Cruelty	Measure of	Refusal to	Feeling of child's
Brutality	trepidation	participate	lack of gratitude
Destructiveness	Feeling of deep hurt		'This won't get you
Stealing (delinquent	'Where will this		anywhere.'
behaviour)	end?'		'It's not up to me to
Bed-wetting	'What will he do		placate or appease
	next?'		you.'
	'What have we done		'You can make the
	to deserve this?'		first move.'
	'How could he		Feeling of self-
	behave like this		justification when
	after all we've		child returns to
	done for him?'		normal
	Feeling of immense		
	relief and hope at		
	any sign of		
	improvement		

Figure 4   Types of Behaviour Classified as Revenge and Parental Reactions to Them

obedience, or delinquency. It is a curious contradiction that a country with compulsory school-attendance laws allows a principal to expel a child with whom the school is unable to deal effectively. Resulting from our failure to view destructive and violent behaviour as a product of discouragement, we push many children into delinquent and criminal behaviour. We must recognise the purpose of revengeful behaviour, sense the deep discouragement, futility, and feelings of worthlessness which characterise these children, and realise that it is always the inability of children to gain a sense of achievement in the home and the school that contributes to their inadequacy.

It is a sad reflection that many adolescents find their only significance in behaviours which are unacceptable to society. Their membership in peer groups which offer exciting activities involving drink, sex, fast cars, drugs, and vandalism is more satisfying than home or school membership. The situation today is aggravated by the many thousands of unemployed youth who feel that they are not wanted by society, by the economy, or by their homes. As a result, they strike out and seek revenge against a community which denies them a place. We must look to means of providing successful, rewarding, and meaningful home and school experiences which counter the child's utter lack of a sense of achievement and the resultant negative self-concept.

Try this

I recently spoke to a group of youth leaders. One leader who was a policeman cited a youth who had been convicted 15 times for car stealing. 'What he needs is stiffer penalties', he maintained.

Do you think that stiffer penalties would have the desired effect?
Why do you think the youth continues to steal cars?
What lies behind his need to steal cars in the first place?

Escape by Withdrawal

The fourth classification of behaviour having an undesirable goal is that in which a child seeks to safeguard prestige by an assumed or real deficiency. These behaviours are referred to as escape by withdrawal and their range, together with parental feeling or reaction, is presented in Figure 5. These behaviours are characterised by a lack of activity, by a submissive or inert attitude, and can be identified by the feeling of helplessness in a parent. Unlike the other three goals, there can be no attacking forms of this behaviour as the child's purpose is to be left alone and to have nothing asked or expected of him.

Children who are deeply discouraged no longer hope for any recognition or success and cease to make any effort. Their sole purpose is to avoid any further hurt, humiliation, or frustration and this is achieved by impressing you with their stupidity. Such children demonstrate hopelessness, stupidity, idleness, inaptitude, indolence, and engage in fantasy activities so that their deficiency will not be so obvious. 'For goodness sake don't ask me to do anything or you will see how hopeless I really am.' A parent who, in despair, throws both hands in the air and declares, 'Timothy, you are hopeless', has been a target of the child's escape by withdrawal behaviour.

CHILD'S GOAL: ESCAPE BY WITHDRAWAL	
	Defending behaviour
Child's strategy	Parent's reaction
'Hopelessness'	Despair
Stupidity	Feelings of futility
Idleness	Feeling of helplessness
Incapability	
Inferiority complex	
Babyish ways	'I just don't know what to do with him.'
Solitary activities	'What can you do with a child like that?'
Refusal to mix	'I give up.'
Fantasy activities	Seizing hopefully upon instances of improved behaviour ('Perhaps he's a late developer')

Figure 5   Types of Behaviours Classified as Escape and Parental Reaction to Them

A side-effect which withdrawal behaviours by children have on parents is to discourage them also. Discouraged children know how to discourage others and the reciprocal discouragement which results ensures that neither parents nor children are able to break the self-fulfilling prophecy of negative expectations.

Such behaviours are usually very effective. When parents are questioned about the range and types of jobs which they expect their son to perform, many will reply, 'I don't ask him to do things any more. He did things so badly that I stopped asking him to do anything.' The child has successfully impressed the parents with his inability and is so excused from further demonstrations of his real or imagined inferiority. Such a child, for example, is not likely to be asked to do the shopping. 'He would buy the wrong things' or 'He would lose the change'. Quite a useful device to employ to avoid any responsibility! Just what do you expect of a child whom you regard as stupid?

Escape behaviour may be complete or partial. It is common for a child to display partial withdrawal in certain areas even though functioning well in others. For instance, a child may do very well at school in English, mathematics, reading, and science but perform poorly in music or art. Most parents and teachers would conclude that the child has little interest or ability in music and art and, in view of the high performance in the other subjects, will excuse the poor result in the other two subjects. In fact, the child's poor performance is not a consequence of limited ability or interest but reflects a child's discouragement in these subjects. A girl whose life style says that she must be the best will not attempt music if she observes that a particular child in her class is already performing well in this area. When the teacher announces that the class will now have music, this particular child will show no interest in participating because she knows that she cannot be the best. This interpretation as 'lack of interest', while understandable, is faulty. She will compete only when she can be the best.

You have all seen an animal use a 'play dead' reflex. Touch a spider and it will curl up as though dead. Children have a similar reflex which may be referred to as a 'play stupid' reflex. Whenever they are asked to do something which they feel is too difficult for them and which might make them look foolish, they put on their 'play stupid' act which excuses their inability to cope. A child keeps the scores very accurately when taken to a rugby match and can quickly convert 2 tries and a penalty into 11 points. However, when asked by the teacher 8 times 6, he fails to respond and puts on an expression which says 'I cannot do mathematics'. By playing stupid, he lowers the teacher's expectation of him and escapes responsibility for making progress in mathematics. Consider the number of adults who gave up mathematics at the first chance they could. They used an assumed inadequacy to escape responsibility. Of course, 'playing stupid' is not confined to children. What would you do if your car broke down this evening? Try to fix it, or put on a display of inadequacy?

Never accept children's display of inability or inadequacy. This is exactly what they want you to do. Children who despair of success, either wholly or partially, are discouraged children who need to be encouraged, who need expression of your confidence in their ability and appreciation of their efforts rather than constant reminders of how poorly they are doing. In a most promising field known as 'mastery learning', Bloom (1976) has obtained very strong evidence to support the thesis, 'What any person can learn, all can learn'. In other words, your child can learn anything and everything. There is no evidence to contradict this statement. When children fail to learn, determine the sources of their discouragement, remove them, and the children will begin to learn again. The 'withdrawal' children are discouraged, not stupid. They have been told so often that they are 'hopeless' that they have come to believe it and act accordingly. They need positive encouragement from their parents and their teachers so that they begin to believe in themselves again, to have their courage restored, and to believe that they can belong through constructive activity.

Try these

(1) Match the feeling on the right-hand side with the goal on the left-hand side.

Child's goal	Child's feeling
A Attention seeking B Power C Revenge D Escape by withdrawal	1 I matter only when I am being noticed. (A)
	2 I'm just no good. There's no use trying. (D)
	3 That will teach you a lesson. (C)
	4 You cannot stop me doing anything. (B)

(2) Which goal?

| A Attention seeking
B Power
C Revenge
D Escape by withdrawal | 1 Clowning
2 Dawdling
3 Shyness
4 'Hopelessness'
5 Defiance
6 Cruelty
7 Incapability
8 Moroseness | (A)
(A)
(D)
(D)
(B)
(C)
(D)
(?) |

Answers

(1) 1 (A); 2 (D); 3 (C); 4 (B)

(2) 1 (A); 2 (B); 3 (A); 4 (D); 5 (B); 6 (C); 7 (D); 8 (C)

4
Identifying the Goals of Misbehaviour

Introduction

In order to assist in the development of children, we need to be aware of the purposes behind their behaviour. Until this is achieved, inadequate forms of behaviour will continue as the goals behind them are obtained. We cannot change a child's behaviour until we are aware of the purpose behind it. What a child does at home, be it acceptable or unacceptable behaviour, represents the manner in which the child has chosen to find a place in the family. Whatever brings desired results, invariably through the reactions of the parents, is continued.

Children who are confident of their ability to find a place, to belong through constructive and co-operative behaviour, will tend not to be a problem. Such children can face the demands of each new situation confident of their ability to cope. However, a child who is discouraged and has lost some self-confidence through practices such as spoiling, overprotection, rejection, punishment, comparison with other children, and fault-finding will turn to unacceptable ways of behaving in order to find a place within the family group.

The previous chapter has classified these unacceptable ways of behaving:

(1) attention seeking: 'I want special recognition and service.'
(2) power: 'You must do what I want.'
(3) revenge: 'I will get even with you.'
(4) escape by withdrawal: 'I am hopeless; leave me alone.'

Parents who are not aware of a child's goals will react in a way which is exactly what the child wants. From the time they get up in the morning until they go to bed at night, children act and parents react. We need to determine which of the four goals the child is displaying and act in such a way to stop reinforcing the child's mistaken belief that belonging is achieved only by obtaining special service, by being the most powerful, the most vicious, or the most hopeless.

It is important to note that the same behaviour may have as its goal any one of the four goals — attention, power, revenge, or withdrawal. Consider a five-year-old girl who is having 'difficulty' in putting on her overcoat. As children of that age can put their coats on without assistance, what is the purpose of her inadequate behaviour? If a parent goes over to assist the child and the child co-operates by offering the coat, sliding easily into it, the goal is clearly attention seeking. She wanted and received special service. If the child's goal is power, she will turn away from the parent and refuse any offer of assistance. If revenge is the purpose, the parent may be the victim of a sharp kick on the ankle. A child who seeks to escape by withdrawal will not refuse the offer of assistance but will be uncooperative with rubber-like arms that will simply not go into the sleeves.

The above example demonstrates that the same behaviour, not putting on a coat, may be directed towards any of the four goals. As each goal requires a different response from parents, how can a parent recognise the purpose behind a child's behaviour? There are two very reliable methods of goal recognition.

How Do You Feel about the Misbehaviour?

An important consideration in relation to the above question is this: 'For whose benefit does a child misbehave?' Parents are clearly unaware that children misbehave at home for the purpose of involving parents. Parents are the targets and their response sustains mistaken goals. 'Why do you keep on annoying me?' is a question posed by a parent who is unaware that the child annoys for the purpose of keeping the parent busy. By examining our own feelings when a child misbehaves, we can determine the purposes of such behaviour.

A child acts knowing how a parent will react. Whatever you feel like doing is exactly what the child wants you to do. Being aware of how you feel about certain behaviours, a child is able to control you. For instance, children who seek attention may show off, eat poorly, fight with siblings, ask incessant questions, or be excessively reliable and co-operative because they know that parents respond predictably to these behaviours. If parents did not respond to them, there would be no point in continuing with them.

How do you feel when a child interrupts your conversation, taps loudly with a fork on a plate, leaves clothes lying around, fights with a younger child, or casually pushes the food around her plate without eating? Annoyance? Right! This is exactly what the child wants you to feel because your annoyance will cause you to react by saying such things as: 'For goodness sake, haven't I told you a hundred times to pick up your toys?' or 'Would you please stop interrupting when I am talking to somebody?' or 'Come on now, I want you to finish all of those vegetables'. Children who believe that they count, only when they are being noticed or served, behave in ways which make you feel annoyed, or want to remind or coax, or feel delighted with 'good' behaviours. By examining your feelings you can readily identify attention-seeking behaviour.

On the other hand, if you feel personally challenged by a child's behaviour and resolve: 'You are not going to get away with that', then power is the goal. A child whose life style is expressed as 'I belong only when I am dominating' is obliged to challenge your power and to make you feel defeated when the child refuses to do what you want him or her to do or engages in acts which are forbidden by you. They argue, contradict, dawdle, throw temper tantrums, and are disobedient, stubborn, and forgetful.

Parents who feel that their authority is being threatened or challenged by a child should recognise the purpose behind the child's behaviour. Children know that you cannot *make* them do anything, and that a child who is able to involve a parent in a power contest has won. There can be no victory for a child if the parent refuses to fight. By openly admitting that we have no special power over children, that we cannot make them do anything and by withdrawing from power contests, we disarm them. Next time you feel angry or that your authority is being threatened, relax, stay friendly, refuse to fight or to be drawn into the contest.

How do we recognise the goal of revenge? A child who operates on this goal feels disliked, rejected, worthless, powerless, and unable to find a useful place in society. As a result, all the child wishes to do is to seek revenge, to hurt and punish that society and those members of society who deny him a place. Their behaviours include stealing, vandalism, and violence — behaviours which greatly dismay and depress parents. If you feel *hurt* by a child's behaviour and ask the question: 'How could you do this to me in view of all the lovely things I have done for you?' then revenge is the goal. While an act of defiance may involve both power and revenge, it is the element of personal hurt which characterises revenge.

How often have we as parents thrown up our arms in a gesture of despair saying: 'I just give up with you Tom'? Convinced that they cannot do anything right and unable to contribute usefully to the family, some children give up trying and use disabilty or inability as an excuse. How do you feel about a child who still cannot add fractions although you have spent four sessions showing him? 'Hopeless.' 'I guess maths is a bit beyond him.' Whenever you feel like that, you can be sure that your child has impressed you with his inadequacy and is operating on the goal of escape by withdrawal. What do you expect of such children? Convinced that they are hopeless, will you send them shopping, ask them to mind the baby, or invite them to set the table? Nothing is expected of these children and nothing is asked of them. They want nothing more than to be left alone and they achieve that by convincing you that they are hopeless.

By examining your own reaction to a child's misbehaviour, you have a reliable guide to the purpose of that misbehaviour. In summary:

If you feel minor annoyance the purpose is attention seeking;

if you feel personally challenged, power;

if you feel deeply hurt, revenge;

if you feel like giving up, escape by withdrawal.

How Does the Child React to Your Correction?

How you feel about a child's misbehaviour is a reliable guide to establishing the purpose of the behaviour. If you would like to check your assessment, a second approach is to observe the children's reaction to your correction.

A boy who seeks attention may sniff constantly while watching television. He is inviting you to correct him. Your minor annoyance may be expressed: 'For goodness sake, stop that sniffing.' His sniffing has successfully made him the centre of attention and he will now cease for the time being as the purpose has been achieved. And so it is with all attention-seeking behaviours. When parents react to them by rebuking, coaxing, threatening, reminding, or punishing, the behaviours will temporarily stop. A little later there will be something else, a fight with a sister, a rude remark, or an annoying habit. And so the day goes on with parents constantly feeding their children's insatiable attention-seeking demands.

While an attention seeker will temporarily desist when given attention, children who operate on the power goal will continue with the disturbing behaviour when reprimanded as their aim is to defeat you. Your correction or demand becomes a signal for the child to intensify the behaviour in an attempt to defeat you. For example, a parent who orders a daughter into her room to 'clean up that mess' will find that the child will not conform to that demand. While she may not openly defy you with 'No, I won't', she just does not get around to tidying up the room. She wants to keep you involved in the game of 'Who wins, who loses?' Your next step is to say, 'Didn't you hear what I said about tidying up that room?' Of course she heard but what she is saying through her passivity is: 'You can't make me do anything.' And so the battle continues until the parent's temper is lost, the child punished, and the lesson learnt: 'Those who have the power win.' Next time the child will be more skilled in using power and will select situations where outright victory is possible.

On those occasions when revengeful behaviour is encountered in the home, parents will find that their reaction to a child's behaviour will cause the child to intensify the struggle and to turn to more violent and vicious forms of attack. By punishing a child for a revengeful act such as stealing or vandalism, parents give the child further reasons for wanting to get even. In addition, the name calling that is associated with revengeful behaviour serves to confirm children's faulty evaluation of themselves. Never regard the revengeful child as 'bad' or 'vicious'; avoid retaliation, maintain order with a minimum of restraint and attempt to communicate to the child that, while the behaviour is not acceptable, the child is.

Punish, rebuke, or indicate your feelings of despair to the children who display escape behaviours and they will bear it all with a martyr-like disposition. They are beyond caring. Convinced of their own inadequacy, children will see parental disapproval and despair as further evidence of their own hopelessness. 'It doesn't matter what happens to me. I am no good.' As parents, we must refuse to accept children's mistaken evaluation of themselves and pursue the long course aimed at restoring and building up their confidence and faith in themselves and in their abilities.

By observing a child's reaction to our correction of his misbehaviour, we have a second reliable guide to identifying the purpose of the behaviour. In summary:

If the child temporarily discontinues the behaviour, the purpose is attention seeking;

if the child continues with the behaviour, power;

if the child shifts to a more violent way of behaving, revenge;

if the child passively endures any punishment, escape by withdrawal.

Having Identified the Goal, What Next?

You are now able to identify the goals towards which misbehaviour is directed. By noting how you *feel* about a child's disturbing behaviour and by observing how the *child reacts* to your correction, you can determine whether the purpose is attention, power, revenge, or escape. For example, a child does not put his toys away. How do you feel? 'Angry.' What did you do? 'Kept at him to do it.' What was his reaction? 'Made only half-hearted efforts to tidy up.' Goal? Power (defending).

One of the most important principles in helping parents deal with misbehaving children is this: 'If you want to change the behaviour of another person, change your own behaviour first.' This is one of the strongest statements in the whole approach of Individual Psychology. Dreikurs (1972:205) has referred to this principle when he wrote:

> If, as you feel weak and hopeless when you are confronted with somebody who doesn't behave properly, you stop thinking about what *he should do*, and begin to think about what *you could do*, the doors open wide. You suddenly become aware of the power which you never dreamt you had. Then you can use encouragement, logical consequences,

persuasion, all these ways for helping him to change — merely by
changing yourself.

Change Own Behaviour First

For parents to change children's behaviour, they must first change
their own. Children misbehave in a home because they know how
parents will react. Whatever parents *feel* like doing is exactly what
children want them to do. Children act while parents react. To break
this cycle, parents must learn to go against their first impulse. First
impulse is always wrong because it is precisely what the child wants
the parent to do and fulfils the expectations of the child who behaves
inappropriately. Dreikurs (1959, 1968) has consistently emphasised
that, before parents can begin to help children, they must stop
behaving inappropriately. As Sweeney (1975:27) writes: 'Behavioural
research on conditioning affirms the Adlerian notion that what most
adults do impulsively when they respond to misbehaviour is incorrect.' Parents must learn to 'catch themselves' and not act
impulsively.

If you have identified the goal as attention seeking, make sure that
the child does not receive attention for this inadequate behaviour. A
boy who is not eating his meal is not urged, coaxed, or fed. As his
poor eating is not a topic for conversation, it now fails as an attention-
seeking device and will be discontinued. A child who dawdles or is
slow or lazy misses out; fighting between children (unless becoming
dangerous) no longer involves parents; a child who misbehaves at a
supermarket does not continue to shop; a child who runs onto the
road stays inside; a child who sleeps-in experiences the consequences
at school; the 'walking question mark' is not answered; the clown is
ignored and fearfulness is kept in very low key. In no case should
the child be reinforced for attention seeking. While you are bound
to feel annoyed and irritated by these behaviours, remind yourself
that the purpose of the behaviours is exactly that — to make you feel
annoyed and irritated. By going against these impulses, you defeat
the purpose of the misbehaviour.

A child who seeks power, loses the fight when the parent refuses
to enter the battle. Having learned to defeat parents by refusing to
do what the parent wants, these children have learned the value of
power. Suddenly it is no longer important as no one will fight.

While parents may feel that their authority is threatened if they
do not make a child obey them, they fail to see that they leave them-

selves vulnerable to the power-conscious child when they attempt to impose their ways upon him. Whether the parent 'wins' or 'loses' is not important to the child; the fact that parents are prepared to fight with the child strengthens the child's belief in the importance of power. He simply becomes more skilful in the exercise of power. A series of endless defeats is in store for parents who believe that they can overpower a 'power-drunk' child. Whenever you feel yourself getting caught up in a power contest, disinvolve, refuse to fight, and remove yourself physically or mentally from the scene of the conflict. You may take the 'wind out of his sail' by admitting that: 'Well I cannot make you do anything.' Such a remark will have a profound effect on a child who believes that he belongs only by being the most powerful. How can you demonstrate your power if nobody will fight with you?

When parents feel hurt by a child's behaviour, they have been the target of revenge. For instance, a mother told me that she wept when her adopted child said to her: 'Why don't you have your own baby so that I can go home to my real parents?' The child sought, successfully, to hurt the mother. Recognise however, that nobody is hurt who doesn't feel hurt; that one is not honoured who doesn't feel honoured; or that one is not humiliated who doesn't feel humiliated. We are in charge of our own feelings and can react to a child's criticism by being hurt or by expressing something like: 'I am sorry that you feel like that.'

Children whose goal is escape through withdrawal have lost confidence in their ability to participate usefully and now wish to be excused from further participation. Parents should never give up with their children and should refuse to accept the child's faulty evaluation. Everything is possible in human behaviour and the task of the parent is to restore confidence in discouraged children, noting improvement, effort, small gains and contribution. Be not impressed by disability or inability and seek to communicate your faith in the child's ability to cope with the problems of living.

It is not sufficient for a parent simply to ignore a child's bid for attention, power, revenge, or escape. Children who consistently disturb or disrupt, or whose behaviour is unacceptable, are discouraged children who believe that they cannot gain a sense of belonging through constructive and co-operative behaviours and consequently turn to inadequate behaviour. The encouragement process holds the key to helping children develop more adequate ways of behaving but, before you can begin to use more positive approaches, you must stop doing those things which strengthen the unacceptable behaviours. As a first step train yourself to go against your first impulse.

Try these

(1) Match the behaviour on the right-hand side with the goal on the left-hand side.

Goal	Behaviour
A Attention seeking B Power C Revenge D Escape by withdrawal	1 'Oh John, how can you be so stupid!' (D)
	2 'For goodness sake, stop that whining.' (A)
	3 'I am not going to tell you again, pick up that coat.' (B)
	4 'I am not going to keep arguing with you.' (B)
	5 'What have we done to deserve this?' (C)
	6 'Doesn't he say the cutest things!' (A)

(2) You have decided that the child's goal is attention seeking. Which of the following actions should you now follow?
   A Attempt to change your child's behaviour so that he no longer seeks attention?
   B Change your own behaviour so that the attention-seeking behaviour is no longer effective?

(B)

(3) How do you feel about a child's misbehaviour? Match these:
   A Attention seeking
   B Power
   C Revenge
   D Escape by withdrawal

   1 Your reaction is anger. (B)
   2 Your reaction is annoyance. (A)
   3 Your reaction is deep hurt. (C)
   4 Your reaction is to give up. (D)

(4) A little revision:

A Attention seeking	1 Clowning	(A)
B Power	2 'Hopelessness'	(D)
C Revenge	3 Stealing	(C)
D Escape by withdrawal	4 Disobedience	(B)
	5 Shyness	(A)
	6 Cuteness	(A)
	7 Stubbornness	(B)
	8 Laziness	(A)

(5) Which parent is most likely to resolve a conflict with a child?
   (A) 'I am not going to tell you again. Get out there and wash your hands'.
   (B) 'I can only serve people with clean hands'.

Answers

(1) 1 (D); 2 (A); 3 (B); 4 (B); 5 (C); 6 (A)

(2) (B)

(3) 1 (B); 2 (A); 3 (C); 4 (D)

(4) 1 (A); 2 (D); 3 (C); 4 (B); 5 (A); 6 (A); 7 (B); 8 (A)

(5) Parent (B) who changed her own behaviour.

5
Encouragement

The Effect of Discouragement on Children

The most important principle which a parent should learn is this: A *misbehaving* child is a *discouraged* child.

Behind all forms of inadequate and disturbing behaviour are discouraged children who feel that, as they are now, they are not much good. To be a child means that you are smaller, weaker, less able, slower, and more inexperienced than all adults and older children. Naturally they cannot do things as well as more experienced parents, older children and siblings. Yet many parents refuse to accept children's current levels of performance and constantly dwell on their imperfections and shortcomings. While all children are capable of improving, our focus on their deficiencies is disastrous and has the effect of providing further discouragement which hinders subsequent improvement.

As a result, many children give up in despair because they feel that they cannot be as good as their parents want them to be or as good as other children. They lose faith in their ability to cope with the learning demands of the various situations and turn to inadequate behaviour in their attempt to salvage some semblance of respect and self-esteem. We all have the power to make some changes in our own behaviour. Each of us can do something about our lives to make them better, to become more effective, to change ourselves. Why don't we? We are discouraged. To help children believe in themselves is the basic task of the parent. Every child who fails to make satisfactory progress in meeting the demands of living — schooling, friendship and neighbourhood, reflects early discouragement and a lack of co-operation in the family.

The basic motivation behind all behaviour is the wish to belong, to feel accepted, to be able to play a constructive role in the group. Only when children feel that they belong to the family, that they are useful and important members of it, can they function adequately, contribute, and co-operate. All initial behaviour of young children is viewed as their attempt to find their place within the family through constructive activity. They will try to feed themselves, to dress themselves, to amuse themselves, and attempt many other tasks which children must learn. If these initial attempts meet with approval from parents, children have the courage and confidence to continue learning and to tackle the more difficult tasks ahead. However, if these initial behaviours of children, imperfect as they must be, meet with frequent criticisms by parents for reasons such as 'too slow', 'too messy', 'not good enough', children begin to lose confidence in their ability to learn the tasks expected of them and turn to various forms of misbehaviour because they believe that they cannot belong through constructive activity.

Many individuals hide their sense of inferiority behind exaggerated superiority. Arrogance, boasting, nagging, deprecating others, intense emotions, not listening, conversation about oneself, exaggerated demands on self or others, vanity and unusual dress — these are signs of inferiority.

All misbehaviour in children has its origin in this basic loss of confidence, in feelings of discouragement, and from the belief that they are not good enough. Children turn to disturbing ways of behaving that will gain them recognition only because they are denied successful learning experiences. Attention, power, revenge, and escape by withdrawal are the only areas open to a discouraged child.

It is important that parents view children's misbehaviour as a product of discouragement rather than as the behaviour of a naughty child, an aggressive child, a lazy child, a spoilt child, or a stupid child. The purposeful nature of these latter behaviours should be clear to you by now but their need arises from a series of discouraging experiences which destroy children's basic belief and confidence in their own abilities. Children are not psychologically sick but are discouraged. By identifying and removing the sources of a child's discouragement we can begin to stimulate a child into more socially acceptable and personally satisfying forms of behaviour.

What Are the Common Sources of Discouragement?

Our present methods of raising children constitute a series of discouraging experiences for many children. Yet, curiously enough, it is the well-intentioned parent who is frequently the major culprit in the discouragement process. Almost without exception, parents are genuinely concerned that their children should become happy and effective individuals but their attempts to attain this result frequently have the opposite effect. Why?

Mistake-centred Approaches

How do parents help children with their social, intellectual, and skill learning? Consider the learning tasks such as making a bed, feeding, building a toy house, dressing, or reading. None of these skills can be acquired quickly and a good deal of imperfection must be expected. Children who are reading poorly lack skill as do children who eat clumsily or dress slowly. Their efforts to learn these tasks, however, represent the means whereby the children can belong to the home through useful activity. As such, they should be strongly encouraged in their learning trials.

Parents invariably react to a child's imperfect performance by pointing out the mistake which the child is making and by showing the correct way of performing or accomplishing the task. They do so because they believe that children will not develop more appropriate ways of behaving unless their errors, deficiencies, slowness, and mistakes are pointed out to them. This sense of responsibility which parents possess is the greatest obstacle in encouraging children's development. It forces parents to act unnecessarily when a child's behaviour is unsatisfactory because parents believe that by chipping away at inadequate behaviour they will be left with a more adequate behaviour. For instance:

If children speak incorrectly, they correct them;

if children use their cutlery wrongly, they correct them;

if children read words wrongly, they correct them;

if children spell words incorrectly, they correct them;

if children make their beds poorly, they correct them.

This focus upon mistakes is calamitous. If you ask parents why they constantly correct children, they will reply that they do not want their children to grow up speaking badly, reading poorly, dressing shabbily, with poor manners, and the like. This attitude, while understandable, constitutes one of the most serious barriers to children's development. It is an attitude which communicates a complete lack of faith in a child's ability and willingness to acquire more adequate behavioural patterns. What the parent communicates is:

'You will continue to be inadequate, deficient, and incorrect unless I point out the error of your ways.'

In life there are always those things which we will do imperfectly. As a fear of being imperfect robs people of their courage, it is necessary that parents communicate to their children, the ability to accept imperfection. We must try to help a child feel good even though he has made a serious mistake or has failed. If we constantly stress perfection, we will always feel inferior because we cannot do things perfectly.

There is nothing wrong in making mistakes. In almost all cases, a mistake represents a lack of skill. Children read, write, spell, or speak poorly because they lack skill at the time. Skill comes with practice and children will practise those activities which they feel confident of their ability to learn. However, if their performance is constantly subjected to well-intentioned criticism, children begin to lose their confidence and believe that they will never learn to read well, write well, cope with mathematics, play games, feed themselves, and the like. A fault-finding attitude has no place in a home. We must communicate to children that we have faith in them so that they have faith in themselves. Avoid approaches which emphasise mistakes in children and shift to those which recognise a job well done, which focus on strengths and assets and which recognise effort. Far too many homes are mistake-centred in which children are made to feel inferior or discouraged if they are not performing adequately. The subsequent loss of confidence and self-esteem is a high price to pay for a parent's lack of wisdom.

Conditional Acceptance

Discouragement comes not only from our concentration upon mistakes or deficiencies, but also from our refusal to accept children as they are and only conditionally upon their being better. Parents constantly impress on children, directly or indirectly, that as they are now they are not good enough because they could do better. This practice is observed in the following examples:

- A young boy begins to take the dishes off the table. 'Oh, no Tim, you might break them. When you are bigger you can do that.'
- A young child makes the bed. 'It is not quite good enough is it? Let me fix it and it will be very nice.'
- A girl wants to carry mother's basket from the market. 'Oh, no

Jill, it's too heavy. When you are a bigger girl you can carry it.'
* A young girl is attempting to dress. 'Oh, Jane, you are so slow. Let
  me do it for you.'

There is only one way in which a child can interpret such remarks.
'As I am now, I am not much good but, when I am bigger, stronger,
faster, and older, I may be all right'. We must accept children as they
are *now* not conditionally on their being better in the future.

Consider how frequently we discourage children by our refusal to
accept them as they are. No matter what they do, there is always
somebody more able, more efficient, more skilful, who will impress
them with their imperfections. A poorly set dinner table which took
a child 20 minutes to complete will be 'fixed' by mother in 20
seconds. Laces, almost tied after five minutes, are tied by a parent in
five seconds. How does it feel to know that everybody is faster,
stronger, and more able? Many children give up because they are
constantly impressed with their inadequacy. How can you improve
when you have lost faith in your ability to improve? Avoid setting
standards which are impossible for children to meet at their present
level of development and accept children as they are. While children's behaviour is always capable of improvement, our conditional
acceptance of children is a major deterrent to any improvement.

Sibling Competition

Competition within the family is another potential source which may
lead to a loss of self-confidence. Parents often highlight differences
between children, praise a successful child, criticise the unsuccessful
one, and by their comparisons, foster competition between children.
As a result, children deny to each other any advantage or benefit and
seek to criticise or deprecate the others in order to gain advantages
for themselves.

In the section which discussed the development of life style, a description was given of the way children establish their own typical
ways of behaving and direct their behaviours towards those ends.
Those qualities or traits will be developed which gain the child a
sense of significance and recognition in the family. Where one child
succeeds, the other will give up; where one shows weakness or
deficiency, the other will demonstrate strength and efficiency. The
greater degree of sibling rivalry, the greater the resulting differences
of personality of brothers and sisters. When there are violent con-
trasts in the personalities of children, we can be fairly sure that there
is a good deal of rivalry in the family. Children, in their intense

competition for attention and power, find ways of achieving these and these ways become what the children are — their personalities.

Within the family, one of the greatest mistakes made by parents is to foster competition among children. Unaware of the reasons for children choosing different ways of behaving, parents are at a loss to understand why one child is scholarly, the other unscholarly; one co-operative, the other unco-operative; one noisy, one quiet; one careful; the other careless. As a result, they accentuate these differences by asking: 'Why can't you be as helpful as your sister?' or 'Why don't you study hard like Paul?'

Parents lose their power to influence when they take sides. Their comparisons strengthen the inadequate behaviours which, from the child's point of view, are working very nicely. 'Parents pay attention to me when I am noisy, untidy, unco-operative, and do poorly at school.' Children influence the behaviour of each other more strongly than do parents. A son convinced that he cannot compete academically with his sister will not apply himself to school even though the parents may admonish, scold, implore, pay for private tuition, supervise homework, and do everything possible to assist with his school work. The ironic aspect is that, if the parents' efforts prove successful and the son does become a successful student, his sister will probably cease to be a successful scholar and will turn to disturbing ways of behaving.

Methods of Training

Parental attitudes and behaviour which are reflected by various methods of child raising are additional sources of discouragement for children. Overprotection, spoiling, overindulgence, and pampering

prevent children from experiencing the consequences of their behaviour, deny them the right to test their strengths or abilities, and to develop independence. Children who are raised in the above manner are always on the receiving end and are never required to contribute or to exercise restraint. As a result they believe that people are there to serve them and to cater to their whims. These children are in for a rude shock when they later learn that the world is not amenable to their wishes, a fact that they are unprepared to accept and one which results in an unresolved frustration, a gift which no parents would want to bestow upon their children.

How to Encourage Children

A previous chapter suggested that parents who attempt to 'correct' a child who is having a particular problem such as eating, dressing, toileting, reading, or speaking will invariably worsen the situation. Why? Because their corrective efforts are invariably directed towards the child's deficiency, inadequacy, or imperfection and, as such, provide an additional source of discouragement for the child. Three ways to encourage children are, to build upon strengths and assets, to emphasise the activity not the result, and to minimise mistakes and deficiencies.

Build upon Strengths and Assets

Consider John, a six-year-old who is having difficulty in learning to read. John knows that he is not doing well because he observes that his classmates read better than he does and that he is frequently reminded by his teacher that his reading is not good enough. As a result, he becomes discouraged in this particular skill. Well-meaning parents observe John reading poorly and receive unfavourable reports from John's teacher concerning his reading. As a result, parents decide to do something about it. Where do they begin? They try to find out what is wrong. Where is the problem? Recognising letters, associating sounds, poor phonic skills, combining sounds, or whatever? They focus on his weaknesses, on his deficiencies. The effect of concentrating on mistakes is to reinforce John's belief that he reads poorly and to provide an additional source of discouragement to an already discouraged child.

Why does John read poorly? Almost all inadequate behaviour of children has a common cause — lack of skill. John lacks skill and will acquire skill through practice. What skills will he practise? Those which he believes he can master; those of which he is confident of his ability to cope. By concentrating on deficiency and on weakness, we erode John's confidence and lead him to believe that he will never be able to read well. It is essential that we begin to focus upon a child's assets and strengths and to minimise mistakes and deficiencies. Never comment negatively on a child's performance.

In the case of John, mother might ask John would he like to read her a short story each night. At the end of each story, mother might

say: 'That's lovely John. Isn't it fun to be able to read such good stories? Tell me, what happened to that little dog you read about? What would it be like to be lost like the little dog?' And so on, both are *enjoying* the reading experience. The many errors which John made during reading are ignored as they reflect lack of skill. John will develop skill as he continues to read, receives instruction at school, and begins to believe that he can cope with the task. Your pleasure in his reading and enjoyment of the activity will build up his confidence and you will find that his reading improves rapidly.

In all children's activities, stay positive and focus on their strengths and assets, no matter how minimal they may be. A painting presented to mother by a kindergarten child might receive the comment: 'What a lovely choice of colours!' not, 'You have drawn the people larger than the house.' A sheet of handwriting, poorly executed, might be greeted: 'Look how well you have done the s's.' Children write and draw poorly because they lack skill and our emphasis on their strengths maintains their confidence to pursue the activities with resultant improvement. Our emphasis on mistakes, no matter how well intentioned, erodes children's confidence and leads them to give up in despair. The enormous number of children requiring remedial education in this country is ample testimony to the stifling effects of discouragement.

Consider a typical mealtime in homes where there are young children. The number of negative or discouraging remarks far exceeds the number of positive or encouraging remarks. Just listen to yourself this evening. 'That's not the way to hold your fork.' 'That's not the way to cut your meat.' 'That's not the way to drink your milk.' 'Take your elbows off the table.' And so the tirade continues. We wrongly believe that by chipping away at bad behaviour we will be left with good behaviour. This will not eventuate as most unsatisfactory behaviours persist *because* of our corrections. As Dreikurs said, what we do to correct children is why they are misbehaving. Parents show little faith in their children when they resort to constant correction. What they are saying in effect is this: 'Unless I correct you, you will remain deficient, inadequate, and unskilful.' Parents who have confidence in their children believe that their children want to improve and will improve provided they have confidence in their ability to do so. In the above example, a parent building on strengths might say: 'Look how well Jim has cut his meat tonight' while disregarding Jim's rather poor attempt at drinking his soup quietly. This latter deficiency will disappear as the child becomes more skilful through practice. By concentrating our remarks on strengths and assets, we assist children to develop the necessary range of skills which result when children have confidence in themselves, a confidence which we as parents must nurture at all costs.

Emphasise the Activity not the Result

There is a strong tendency in children, particularly first-born, to evaluate themselves in terms of their achievement. They identify what they *do* with what they *are*. Such children will complete a task for the sole purpose of winning parental praise as they believe that they belong only when their achievements are approved of by others. A parent's praise becomes a reward and some children feel worthwhile only when their performance attracts such a reward. This particular belief is fostered by parents who focus on the product of an activity rather than on the activity itself. A father who asks his son: 'How many goals did you score today?' or 'How many runs did you make?' is focusing on the product rather than the activity. How does a child feel who thoroughly enjoyed the game but who kicked no goals or made no runs? *A failure*. Why? Because the father has communicated the following message: 'You belong only when you are kicking goals or making runs.'

Some time ago, I witnessed a pony club event in which children were required to plot a jumping course and execute the jumping against the clock, the winner being the child who scored the most points within the time prescribed. Plotting a careful course is the key to the event as the jumps have different point values. As soon as the values were announced, one couple ran out with a calculator and a graph pad and did the necessary calculations, a task which belonged to the child. They returned to their seven-year-old, taught him the 'ideal' course, and off he went. He jumped well apart from one obstacle which he dislodged, an error which cost him the ribbon. As he returned to his parents, they turned away and began a conversation with acquaintances. The child dismounted, removed the helmet, and tears were visible. What had the parents said to him through their behaviour? 'Winners belong in this family and as you are not a winner, you do not belong.'

Our emphasis upon the end product of an activity will cause many children to give up because they cannot do as well as others want them to do, or they will not attempt activities because they cannot be the best, or they will not finish projects because they cannot be completed perfectly. Children take on many activities but fail to complete any because they believe that nothing they can do is good enough. Children's acceptance or belonging within a family must be unconditional and not dependent upon their getting the highest marks at school, making the most runs, winning the athletics event, a blue ribbon, or being the best. Children belong by virtue of what they *are* not by virtue of what they *do*. We fail to communicate this acceptance when we focus on the result of an activity. High achievement in children is to be encouraged. However, a child's belonging in a family should never depend upon high achievement. The message parents should give their children is this: 'You are totally acceptable as you are now. If you want to be a high achiever, good. But you belong, irrespective of the outcome.'

It is a better procedure to concentrate on the activity itself or the contribution rather than on its outcome. For example, a child who comes home from a basket-ball game and remarks: 'I threw 16 points today' might receive a reply from a parent: 'I am glad that you enjoyed the game.' Elevate the status of the *activity* of playing rather than the *product* of playing. A child who brings home a school report card which has all A's might receive a comment such as: 'I am pleased to see you enjoy learning. You must feel good when you enjoy what you are doing.' Learning is the activity which contributes to the A's and by acknowledging that we shift the emphasis away from the feeling of the child, 'I belong only if I continue to be best in school.' The stress is on what the child is doing rather than on the child.

Consider the following example. A parent asks a child to help clean up the kitchen. The child does so and the parents say: 'Great job. I have never seen the kitchen looking so clean.' Was this a good procedure? No, because it focused on the end product. What might the parent have said? 'Thanks for your help in cleaning up the kitchen. It makes my job so much easier.' All children can contribute but they cannot all be the best. What would the child think next time he/she cleans up the kitchen and the parent does not comment? 'I didn't do it so well that time. I didn't please my parent.'

A type of child for whom this principle of encouragement is particularly important is the over-ambitious child. Such children set impossibly high goals for themselves because they feel that they have to be the best. As a result, they fail to finish things because they cannot do them well enough (perfectionism) or they do not make any effort when they feel they cannot be the best (over-ambition). When the goal is to be the best, to be perfect, discouragement is inevitable, be it in children or parents.

The effect of frustrated over-ambition may be seen in the case of a child who brought home a painting which he had completed at school. When his mother remarked: 'What a lovely painting Tom!' he tore the painting in half, threw it to the floor, and went outside. What went wrong? Tom is a perfectionist and judges himself against what he *does*. However, because he is such a perfectionist, nothing he can do is ever good enough. He became angry when mother praised his painting because it indicated to him that even she did not understand what a failure he was. If mother had concentrated on the activity and said, 'I see that you enjoy painting', she would have shifted the emphasis away from the product to the activity, from the actor to the act. Recognise the *act* not the *actor*, the *activity* not the *product*, the *contribution* not the *result*.

Linked to this discussion is the distinction between praise and encouragement. Many parents believe that by praising children they will stimulate them into appropriate behaviour. In fact it is likely to have the opposite effect. Praise is usually reserved for things well done and is interpreted by children as meaning that *they* have measured up to the demands and values of *others*. If children do not receive praise, they may assume that they have not measured up to the standards of others or that what they have to offer is not worth the effort.

Praise always involves the child rather than the child's behaviour. Praise rewards the individual rather than the individual's effort or act. Praise is only offered for well-done acts rather than for effort or improvement. Praise teaches the child to compete in order to receive praise rather than to contribute because the situation requires it. Typical statements of praise and their equivalents in encouragement are:

Praise	*Encouragement*
1 'I am so pleased that you topped the maths test'.	1 'I am so pleased that you are enjoying maths'.
2 'I have never seen your room looking so tidy'.	2 'Thank you for tidying up your room. It makes my job easier'.
3. 'You are such a good boy, Jim'.	3 'Thanks for putting the messages away. It was a big help'.

In summary, encouragement recognises effort and improvement, shows appreciation for contributions, accepts children as they are *now*, recognises the activity, and focuses on strengths. Praise is an external reward, given only for well-done tasks, focuses upon the individual, and teaches that to be worthwhile the child must measure up to the demands and values of others.

Minimise Mistakes and Deficiencies

Many parents place too much importance upon avoiding mistakes either in their children or in their own behaviour. This attitude is the residue of an autocratic society which established absolutes in 'rights' and 'wrongs' and viewed mistakes as nonconformity with the demands of society.

> As long as you do as I tell you there is no mistake possible because I am right. I say so. Making a mistake therefore means that you have not done what I told you. And I won't stand for that. (Dreikurs, n.d.)

In today's society there are no absolutes. Absolutes are possible only if we have an authority which decides what is right and wrong. Today, the principles of mutual respect, social equality, and self-determination imply that each of us personally decides what is right and wrong, true or false, and evaluates our behaviour against those judgments.

We live in a 'mistake-centred' society in which people are afraid to make mistakes. Part of this attitude may be accounted for by the traditions of the past where mistakes implied nonconformity, a subordinate role, and an element of worthlessness. Today, it may be explained as the fear of losing one's status. In a competitive society such as ours where people are uncertain of their belonging, where many individuals feel that they have to be better than others, or have more wealth, power or status, people are desperately trying to be right all the time because of the ridicule, the humiliation, and the loss of status which mistakes incur. As a result, people make every effort to avoid mistakes, an attitude which invariably leads to mistakes. When we focus on error, we discourage ourselves and are subsequently led into error. The greatest motivation for doing something wrong is discouragement. Further, when we expect to behave in a certain way, there is a strong tendency to confirm that expectation. If we expect to make mistakes, we probably will.

Our emphasis upon mistakes in children is self-defeating. When we warn children about the possibility of making mistakes in an activity, it is almost certain that they will make them. By alerting them to the possibility of an error, we discourage them by decreasing their self-confidence. A child who is writing out birthday invitations should not be subjected to 'Careful now, no spelling errors' or 'Only your best writing now'. Mistakes under these circumstances are highly likely and are the result of our communicating to the child that we *expect* poor spelling or poor writing.

There is nothing wrong in making mistakes. In many learning situations they are unavoidable — ask any golfer. Children who are afraid of making mistakes cannot function effectively because the only time they know whether they are right or wrong is *after* an activity. If they are afraid of making mistakes, they cannot move, develop, or make decisions because they are afraid that they may be wrong. Children need to learn that there is nothing wrong in making mistakes, that mistakes are useful learning experiences, and that it is more important to decide what to do after the mistake is made than to avoid making the mistake. Letting children try to do things for themselves makes them responsible.

Remember, mistakes reflect a lack of skill which will be remedied as long as children have confidence in their own ability. Do not erode this confidence by mistake-centred approaches. Centre children's attention on the things which they have done well, focus on strengths, recognise effort, and minimise mistakes, and you will find that the faults of children, which are currently fostered by discouragement, will become fewer and fewer. The training and education of children must shift from a mistake-centred approach to an achievement-centred one which acknowledges the contribution of children and communicates our faith in their ability to become responsible and independent individuals.

Try these

(1) Sally, nine years, and her younger sister, Ruth, seven years, both came home from school and presented their parents with the following report cards:

	Sally	Ruth
Maths	A	D
English	A	D
Social Studies	A	D
Art	A	C
Science	A	D

Which of the following conclusions are warranted from your reading of this chapter?

		Yes	No
1	Ruth's poor marks are a result of discouragement.	....	...✓...
2	Sally is a major source of Ruth's discouragement.	...✓...	....
3	Parents could motivate Ruth by comparing her results with those of Sally.	....	...✓...
4	Parents might usefully say to Ruth: 'We are so pleased to see that you enjoy Art. It's a fun subject, isn't it?'	✓	....
5	Parents should praise Sally by saying: 'We are so pleased that you obtained all A's.'	....	...✓...
6	Parents should say to Sally: 'We are so pleased to see that you enjoy learning.'	✓	....
7	Parents should try to find out why Ruth is doing poorly and arrange for private tuition.	....	✓
8	Evidence suggests that this is a co-operative family.	....	✓
9	Ruth will not improve her grades unless Sally is prepared to change her attitude.	....	✓

(2) Read the sentences on the right-hand side. Which principle on the left-hand side is relevant?

---

1 Build upon strengths and assets.	A. 'Why don't you work as hard as your sister?' (3)
2 Emphasise the activity not the result.	B. 'I am so pleased to see that you obtained all A's.' ( )
3 Avoid competition between children.	C. 'I am so pleased to see that you enjoy studying.' (2)
4 Discouragement is a major source of poor performance.	D. 'I think you use colour very well in your Art.' (2)
	E. 'I expect that you have done poorly again Ruth?' (4)

---

(3) John was building a model 'plane. He couldn't make the wings stay on firmly. He asked his father for help. Father said, 'You are using the wrong glue; try the other cement. But really, the wheels and tail-piece are so poorly cut out that they spoil the 'plane. Take them off and trim them.'

   (a) What mistakes did father make?
      (i)
      (ii)

   (b) What should father have said or done?
      (i)
      (ii)
      (iii)

(4) Which of the following statements give praise and which give encouragement?
   (a) 'That is a difficult problem but I am sure that you will work it out.' E
   (b) 'I was so proud when you won the race.' P
   (c) 'Your room really is tidy now.' P
   (d) 'I see that you have worked hard on that model.' E
   (e) 'Thanks for taking out the rubbish. It makes my work easier' E
   (f) 'Nine out of ten is pretty good result. Aim for ten next time!' P

Answers

(1) Yes; 2 Yes; 3 No; 4 Yes; 5 No; 6 Yes; 7 No; 8 No; 9 Yes

(2) 1 (D); 2 (C); 3 (A); 4 (E)

(3) (a) (i) He focused on the child's deficiency.
      (ii) He discouraged by highlighting the poorest aspects of the model.

   (b) A better approach for father would be:
      (i) Enter enthusiastically into the project:
         'This is a fine 'plane.'
      (ii) Show John how to use the new cement.
      (iii) Comment on the better parts of the model:
         'You have done a great job on the engine.'

(4) (a) Encouragement: shows confidence
    (b) Praise: pleases by meeting external standards
    (c) Praise: given only for well-done tasks
    (d) Encouragement: recognises effort
    (e) Encouragement: acknowledges a contribution
    (f) Praise: given only for well-done tasks

6

A New Approach to Child Discipline — Rewards and Punishments or Behavioural Consequences

Rewards and Punishments

Discipline in the home and the school has become a major problem and increasing numbers of parents and teachers report their inability to effectively manage children. We have become so accustomed to difficult children and adolescents that many now regard their behaviour as normal and attribute the problem to various economic, cultural, political or social factors. Many of the authorities in the field of child behaviour pronounce on the causes and treatment, making recommendations which are likely to exacerbate rather than ease the problem. This is particularly true when the use of rewards and punishment are advocated. The use of rewards and punishments as a means of controlling behaviour has been with us for such a long time that parents have come to accept it as inevitable. Parents who continue with the use of rewards and punishments will find that these techniques create greater problems than those which their use was designed to correct. Pressure from without, utilising the reward-and-punishment method, has lost its effectiveness and needs to be replaced by approaches which emphasise internal control and the personal responsibility of the individual.

Rewards and punishments are products of the authoritarian system which reaffirmed the traditional superiority of one group over another. Those in the superior position, the parents for instance, made all decisions about how their children would behave and used rewards and punishments to enforce compliance. 'Because you have done what I wanted you to do, I will reward you' is the message behind the behaviour of a parent who buys a child an icecream for sitting quietly in the car or pays a child to rake up the leaves. Similarly, a smack on the bottom or the loss of privilege carries the message: 'Because you have *not* done what I wanted you to do, I will punish you.' There is no question that rewards and punishment were useful in an autocratic society but, as society changed, so did the usefulness and desirability of these disciplinary methods.

With the passing of the authoritarian system and its replacement by a democratic society, the vertical continuum of superiority-inferiority gave way to a system of social equality and mutual respect. With the advent of democracy, previously suppressed groups such as women, children, coloured races, and the poor have new status and rights, rights which provide for self-determination and self-direction of behaviour.

Within such a society, the use of rewards and punishments is inappropriate and ineffective. While rewards and punishments may temporarily alter specific behaviours, they do not teach self-confidence, self-discipline, self-reliance nor do they encourage contribution or creativity. We reward our inferiors when they do what we want them to do; we punish our inferiors when they do not do what we want them to do. Among social equals, rewards and punishments have no validity. Do you really know what is best for others? Do you have the right to make others behave in certain ways? In an autocratic society, yes; in a democratic society, no. Parents have a responsibility to teach their children appropriate behaviours but they do not have the right to impose behaviours on children.

Not only are rewards and punishments inappropriate in today's society, but they are no longer effective. The use of punishment will create a number of problems such as:

(a) Punishment has the effect of inviting retaliation. A parent who smacks a boy for hitting his sister and then sends him to his room may find that the boy scribbles all over the wallpaper. What he is saying is: 'If you have the right to hurt me, I have the same right to hurt you.' Revenge and retaliation are characteristic of children who are controlled by punishment.

(b) Punishment has the effect of temporarily suppressing behaviour but not of eliminating it. A parent who punishes a child for coming home late from school will find that, for a short time, the child will come home on time. But observe the child a few weeks later and you will find that the punished behaviour returns to strength. More punishment will again temporarily suppress the lateness. The principle is clear; if you are going to control by punishment you must keep on punishing. Is that the way you want to raise children? To behave correctly only because of the threat of punishment?

(c) The use of punishment requires that the parents assume the responsibility for their children's behaviour. Rather than allowing children to make decisions and accept responsibility for those decisions, parents do all the deciding about dressing, meals, manners, bedtime, speech, and so on, using punishment as a way to suppress the behaviours which they regard as undesirable for children. It is little wonder that so many children are irresponsible when they have not been required to experience the consequences of irresponsibility.

(d) The use of punishment invites resistance as children, whose goal is power, refuse to do what parents want. Try to make children tidy their rooms, complete homework, take out the rubbish or pick up toys and they will fight you. No amount of punishment will deter such children whose purpose it is to defeat you. The use of punishment only helps children to develop greater powers of resistance and defiance and to challenge parents in a manner and degree which were unthinkable in past generations.

Rewarding children for acceptable behaviour is just as detrimental as punishing them. Like punishment, reward is a product of a system which assumes that others know what is best for individuals and rewards them when they conform. Children raised under such a system soon develop a 'What's in it for me?' attitude and will refuse to participate unless they are rewarded. 'Would you like to mow the lawn, John?' 'How much?' Children come to believe that they have

a right to be rewarded and will not do anything unless a reward is promised. If ever you require children to do something for which they are not rewarded, they will punish you. No matter whether you are using rewards or punishments you are likely to end up being punished by children either through revenge or retaliation.

Not only do rewards fail to develop responsibility in children (it is the parent's responsibility to induce 'good' behaviour by promising a reward), but their use serves to discourage children. A mother who leaves her two small children with a friend while she goes shopping may say to them: 'If you behave while I am away, I will bring each of you a packet of Smarties.' This use of reward is a form of discouragement, for what mother is really saying is: 'I know that you are usually naughty and won't behave, but if you will be different (i.e. 'good') this time, I will reward you.' Children do not need to be rewarded to act responsibly; they prefer to belong and contribute through useful, helpful, responsible, and co-operative behaviour. We should respect and capitalise on this desire by providing opportunities for its expression rather than distorting it by offering rewards or threatening punishment.

Is there an alternative to rewards and punishments which is more effective and relevant to the democratic climate which is beginning to characterise our homes? The technique of behavioural consequence has many advantages over rewards and punishments and none of the unfortunate consequences. It is one of the most important techniques parents can use to teach their children to be responsible for their behaviour and to improve relationships with their children.

Behavioural Consequences

We would like our children to behave responsibly and appropriately, not because of fear of punishment or promise of reward, but because they come to a decision that certain ways of behaving are more satisfying than others. We aim to induce responsible behaviour not by pressure from above but by stimulation from within. That is, children will decide to behave in a particular manner, not because we demand it but because they come to a realisation that it is a better way of behaving. How do we achieve this aim?

The most powerful technique which is available to parents to stimulate responsible behaviour is the use of behavioural consequences. The basis of this approach is that all behaviour is shaped and maintained by its consequences and that individuals will not continue to behave in ways which distress only themselves. No person will willingly do what he believes is harmful to himself. Why is it that children learn to respect a hot stove, a sharp knife, a slippery rock, a snarling dog, or a bicycle that tilts too far to the side? It is because they always experience the consequence of their behaviour — they are burnt, cut, bitten, or hurt. Who brings these consequences about? Children do, by behaving inappropriately. As a result they quickly learn more skilful means of coping with these situations, learning which has required no parental interference and no use of external rewards or punishments. These are two types of behavioural consequences.

Natural Behavioural Consequences

The consequences are a product of the natural environment and do not require the intervention of another person. For instance, a child who refuses to eat becomes hungry; a child who leaves off a warm jacket in winter becomes cold; a child who puts shoes on the wrong feet will have toes pinched; a child who stays up late at night will be tired the next day.

Logical Behavioural Consequences

These consequences result from activities within the social rather than the natural environment and require the intervention of another person, usually an adult. A child who gets up late in the morning will experience the consequence of lateness at school; a lunch-box left home remains at home; a cricket bat left outside and stolen is not replaced; library books not returned deny to the borrower the right to use the library; a child who slaps a baby sister is not allowed to play in her room; a child who does not practise is not selected in the team, while children who come in late for meals miss out.

Many parents find it difficult to differentiate between punishment and behavioural consequences. Here are several important differences:

Punishment	Behavioural Consequences
1 Parent is responsible for the child's behaviour.	1 Children are responsible for their own behaviour.
2 Parents decide what a child will do.	2 Children decide their own course of action.
3 Expresses the power of the parents.	3 Express the reality of the natural or social order.
4 Involves no element of choice for the child.	4 Provide children with choices.
5 Unrelated to the particular behaviour.	5 Logically related to the behaviour.
6 Is always personalised and implies a moral judgment.	6 Impersonal and involve no moral judgment.
7 Concerned with the past and is retaliatory.	7 Concerned with the present or future and are non-retaliatory.

The following examples may help clarify the differences between punishment and behavioural consequences.

Punishment	Behavioural Consequences
1 'Because you have not tidied up after you, you get no pocket-money this week.'	1 'Because I have not tidied up after me, I cannot find anything.'
2 'You will eat what I tell you to eat.'	2 'If I don't eat, I will get hungry.'
3 'Turn off that radio, I am trying to read.'	3 'You can stay here as long as the volume is down. Otherwise go outside and play.'
4 'Come in here and put on that jumper.'	4 'If I don't put my jumper on I get cold.'
5 'Because you did not sweep up the leaves, you cannot watch TV tonight.'	5 'Because you stayed up so late last night, you would not enjoy the drive-in tonight.'
6 'You played my record without permission and scratched it. You just don't care about other people's things. I am going to punish you.'	6 'I see that my record is scratched. How do you propose to replace it?'
7 'You said that you would mow the lawns today. You didn't. Just forget about our trip to the snow next weekend.'	7 'I see that you didn't clean up after your snack. You may not use the kitchen. Ask again in a few days' time.'
8 'You are home late again. Why don't you think of others? You go to bed straight after dinner.'	8 'I am sorry that you missed dinner. It was served at 6.'

Applying Behavioural Consequences

The use of consequences can best be demonstrated by considering their application to a number of common family problems. Remember that we are not trying to force a child do anything nor are we demanding particular behaviours. Rather, we are allowing children freedom to behave in certain ways and ensuring that they experience the consequences of their behaviour. The *only* exception is when physical danger is involved, such as in crossing a road. It is not that strong, punitive, or dominating adults are arbitrarily imposing their values on children; on the contrary. Our role as parents is almost that of a neutral bystander who, when a child complains about a particular consequence, for example, being hungry after not eating at mealtime, takes the position: 'I am sorry that you are hungry but you know what to do about it.' We would like our children to adopt certain behavioural patterns, not because we demand that they do but because they come to a realisation that certain ways of behaving are more satisfying than others. In this way, we teach children responsibility. The consequences of reality impress the child rather than the power of the adult.

Getting Children up in the Morning

Most of our lives are organised around time, and nowhere is this more apparent than in the early morning routine of a home where individuals must leave for work and school at regular intervals. Many children use this time to put parents into their service, to violate order, and to engage in other attention-seeking behaviours. The use of behavioural consequences is the most effective technique to employ to establish responsible behaviour by children. Consider the following example of a typical home situation.

> Mother has great difficulty in getting Sandra out of bed in the morning. She has to call her at least three or four times before she gets out of bed. Sandra is a slow dresser; she has to be called often to come to breakfast; her eating of breakfast is haphazard and invites frequent parental comment; and on many occasions she has to be driven to school in order not to be late.

What should mother do? She should use behavioural consequences and allow Sandra to experience the consequence of her behaviour.

Mother's responsibility is to wake Sandra in the morning and to provide breakfast at a particular time. There her responsibility ends. She must not take over the responsibility which rightly belongs to her daughter. How can we teach children responsibility if we do not require them to behave responsibly? Having been woken, it is Sandra's responsibility to rise and dress. She is not called again. Breakfast is served at, say, 7.45 a.m. and, if Sandra is not there, she misses out. If she is there and dressed at 7.45 a.m., she is served but no comment is made about her departure deadline slipping by as she dawdles through breakfast. Sandra must walk to school even though she is going to be late.

That evening when Sandra comes home and complains to mother that she got into trouble at school because she was late, mother's approach is: 'I am sorry that you got into trouble at school but you know what to do about it.' Responsibility is placed where it belongs, with Sandra. No one is going to *make* her get up, eat quickly, or leave on time. It is her responsibility to organise herself in the morning and she will do this if she experiences the consequences of disorder. Too many parents take over the responsibilities of their children and wonder why their children are so irresponsible. We encourage children in responsible behaviour by allowing them to experience the consequences of irresponsible behaviour.

Misbehaviour Outside the Home

Many family outings begin with a happy expectation and end up as a disaster. Look at an average family setting out eagerly for a day at the Royal Agricultural Show. Contrast their departure with their return — a day when children have made an enormous number of unreasonable demands, parents have become short-tempered, children have whined and complained, and everybody is on edge, disillusioned, and thankful that it is all over. Must outings with children end up like this? Must a visit to a restaurant by a family be the occasion for children to display their worst behaviour? Must shopping expeditions be marred by constant demands by children for sweets, ice-cream, and toys, with resultant displays of temper when these demands are denied? The use of consequences is the most powerful training technique available to parents to induce responsible behaviour in children.

Supermarket Visits

When mother takes Jenny to the supermarket, she knocks groceries off the shelves, opens packets of lollies, and pushes her trolley into other people. Mother admonishes, scolds, bribes — all to no avail as Jenny continues on her irresponsible way.

Mother should not comment on the child's misbehaviour but quietly and firmly say: 'I see that you are not prepared to come shopping with me today' and both Jenny and mother return home immediately. Mother then shops alone. Jenny is told to tell mother when she is prepared to go shopping again. Three days later, Jenny asks mother if she can go shopping with her. She is saying, in effect, 'I am prepared to behave at the supermarket.' If Jenny repeats any of her antics, the same procedure is repeated. She will quickly learn that when she goes shopping with mother she behaves herself. If she does not, she misses out. It is up to her. Nobody is going to *make* her behave but, when she misbehaves, she experiences the consequences of her misbehaviour. Concentrate on the principle behind this example rather than on the difficulty involved in who might mind your child while you do the shopping. The latter can usually be resolved by involving a co-operative neighbour, friend, or relative.

Visiting Friends

Harold is not an easy boy to take visiting. He fights with the other children, damages their toys and seems to enjoy the embarrassment which he causes his parents. Mother tries to control him by suggestions and threats — all to no avail. 'Visiting friends is hardly worthwhile when Harold is like this', says mother to father.

What should parents do? The child has to learn that when he goes visiting with his parents he behaves himself. When they go to a friend's house, parents do not tell Harold what he must do or what he must not do. They extend freedom and do not attempt to dominate him. If Harold behaves poorly by hitting another child, a parent should say: 'I see that Harold does not feel like visiting today' and they all go home immediately. This is the consequence of disturbing behaviour. Nobody is making Harold do anything but, when he chooses to behave in certain ways, he finds that he misses out. It does not require more than one or two of these experiences before Harold learns acceptable ways of behaving. From then on, the family will enjoy going out together because they can rely on their children to behave responsibly.

Running onto the Road

You should now be able to apply the above principles to the child who endangers himself by running onto the road when he is playing outside. 'I see that you are not prepared to play outside. You tell mother when you are ready to do so.' The child is immediately taken inside.

Notice that no comment is made about the actual behaviour, the running onto the road. Never tell a child what he already knows. Act and keep verbal remarks to a minimum. When this child approaches his mother in a day or so and says that he is prepared to play outside, what he is saying is that he is prepared not to run onto the road.

Damage to Belongings of Others

John took his father's saw to school without obtaining permission. He damaged the teeth. Father might say: 'I see you have damaged my saw. Would you like to have it repaired out of your pocket money or would you like to earn some extra money to pay for it?'

A choice is given; the consequence is impersonal involving no blame; the consequence is logically related to the behaviour; and the tone of voice is friendly and matter-of-fact. John will be more responsible next time.

Failure to Pick up Toys

Alan leaves his toys lying around the house and is 'mother deaf' to her repeated demands that he pick them up. Mother might decide that the toys are interfering with her work and therefore pick them up. However, she will put them in a cupboard where Alan is unlikely to find them. When he asks, 'Where is my boat?', Mother might respond, 'Well, where did you leave it?', 'I don't know.' 'Well, when we leave things lying around it is always hard to find them.' The boat does not appear for two weeks.

Alan will learn that the consequence of leaving toys lying around is that they are lost.

Behaviours Which Violate Order

Sam likes to play football and frequently comes home late for dinner which is served at 7 p.m. His parents rebuke him for his lateness and he is sometimes punished. His punctuality does not improve. Mother should use consequences. Next time Sam comes home late after kicking a football in the paddock, mother might say: 'I am sorry you missed out on dinner. It was served at 7.'

What is mother making Sam do? Nothing. It is perfectly all right for him to kick a football at all hours but he must experience the consequence of his behaviour, that is, he misses dinner. He has freedom to decide what he will do but, when he violates order, he experiences the consequences. In this manner Sam will learn respect for order.

Eating Problems

June is a poor eater and has to be reminded, coaxed, and cajoled into eating despite the fact that mother frequently cooks June's favourite foods and has a special dessert for her at the end of dinner as a reward. Mother should use natural behavioural consequences. Food is presented and no comment is made about June's eating. Those who finish their first course receive 'seconds'. June, who is not eating her first course, is presumed to be 'not hungry' and receives no second. At the end of the meal, all dishes are removed. Nothing has been said to June about her poor appetite. The consequence is that June will become hungry; when she complains to mother about her hunger, mother might say: 'I am sorry that you are hungry, but you know what to do about it.'

Natural consequences will soon ensure that the eating problem is overcome.

Some parents may feel that the use of consequences imposes unnecessary pain or discomfort on their children. For instance, the child who does not eat his dinner goes to bed hungry; the child who leaves his sweater at home is cold all day; or the child who leaves his bike out in the street loses it. While they are uneasy about a child inflicting pain upon himself, they have no such uneasiness when they spank the child, punish him, deprive him of pleasures, or other such aversive measures which have characterised parental control. Parents rationalise such punitive behaviour by saying 'It is good for the child' but behind these parental behaviours is the attempt to dominate, to have the child do what they want. In other words, parents have a stake in the child's eating, getting up, going to bed, and so on. They are personally involved and want their children to behave as they want them to.

This is the conflict today. Parents are saying through their behaviour:

'You will get up when I tell you to get up.'

'You will eat what I tell you to eat.'

'You will not watch what I tell you not to watch.'

'You will go to bed when I tell you to go to bed.'
Children are saying through their behaviour:
'I will get up when I want to get up.'
'I will eat what I want to eat.'
'I will watch what I want to watch.'
'I will go to bed when I want to go to bed.'
Many homes are deadlocked in power struggles. Parents need to remove themselves from the role which attempts to dominate children and begin to use behavioural consequences to induce satisfactory behaviour.

With the advent of democratic ways of living and the acceptance of the principle that we deal with each other as social equals, our right to dominate children has gone. The use of consequences allows parents to withdraw from the conflict situations and adopt an attitude of neutral concern. Their children's behaviour produces consequences which are not imposed by parents but which stem from the natural or from the social environment. Children see that nobody is making them do anything, that they are free to behave as they choose but that they experience the consequences of their behaviour. The consequence is not the whim of a parent, but the result imposed by an environment which presents rules for living which all individuals must learn if we are to live together effectively. We respect a child's right to decide but ensure that the consequence of the choice is experienced. Permissive parents do not let children experience consequences; autocratic parents do not let children make a decision.

Democratic parents teach self-discipline by utilising behavioural consequences.

One final word about the use of behavioural consequences. When using this technique, you must be matter-of-fact and non-punishing, genuinely unconcerned and not involved with the child's unsatisfactory behaviour. It really is not your business whether a child gets up on time, completes homework, puts things away, or eats heartily. The responsibility for those actions rests with the child. If, however, you express concern, a battle results which both parent and child are determined to win. In such a situation, the use of consequences is impossible. One reliable guide to your level of involvement is your tone of voice. If your tone is harsh, critical, or demanding, you are clearly personally involved and are caught in a power contest no matter what you are actually saying. If your voice is friendly, firm, and kind, often expressing regret, 'I am sorry that you cannot find your train set . . .', then you are probably not involved with the problem and the way is clear for the use of behaviour consequences.

Test your skill

(1) Your daughter has agreed to take the rubbish out of the kitchen every evening and put it in the outside bin. She fails to do so on Wednesday night. A consequence of her behaviour might be:

   A. Mother scolds the child and makes her take it out.
   B. Mother takes it out but doesn't let her daughter watch TV that night.
   C. Mother leaves the rubbish in the kitchen but decides not to cook breakfast next morning because the kitchen is so offensive.

(2) Your child, aged 4, puts his shoes on the wrong feet and complains about the discomfort. Your reaction should be:

   A. Ignore the child's complaint that his toes are being pinched and say, 'I am sorry but you know what to do about it.'
   B. Say, 'Come here silly. You have your shoes on the wrong feet' and then put them on correctly for him.

(3) Robert, aged 7, opens packets of sweets at the supermarket. Mother finds him taking a jelly-bean out of a packet which he has just taken off the shelf. What should she say?

A. 'How many times have I told you that money doesn't grow on trees. Those lollies cost Mummy 20p. You naughty boy.'

B. 'I see you want to purchase the sweets. Do you have your pocket money with you or will I lend you 20p until you get home?'

C. 'You naughty boy. You put those right back. That is the same as stealing'.

(4) Which parent is using behavioural consequences?
   (i) Parent A: 'Pick up those toys. I am sick of the living room being untidy.'

        Parent B: 'I wouldn't know where to put the clean clothes in your room. I will leave them on the chair outside.'

  (ii) Parent A: 'If you don't stop that arguing, there will be no television.'

        Parent B: (Having turned the TV set off) 'You tell me when you have decided which program you will watch.'

 (iii) Parent A: 'I am sorry that you couldn't play. You might remember your equipment next time.'

        Parent B: 'It serves you right. You don't deserve to play if you forget your equipment.'

(5) The most responsible children in this world are those who have seriously ill mothers. What lesson can be learned from this?

Answers

(1) C

(2) A

(3) B

(4) (i) B; (ii) B; (iii) A

(5) Children were required to accept responsibility. They were given the opportunity to contribute to the welfare of the family.

7
Improving Parent–Child Relationships

A number of approaches have been outlined which are designed to improve the relationship between parents and their children. When parents are able to avoid the fallacy of the first impulse and can successfully use encouragement approaches and behavioural consequences, there should be a significant improvement in the behaviour of children and the beginning of the development of confident, responsible, co-operative and independent children.

The skills which are described in this chapter are complementary to the above techniques and are consistent with the philosophy previously expressed that parent-child relationships, in a democratic society, should be characterised by mutual respect, social equality, co-operation, and shared responsibility. Gone are the days when parents knew what was 'best' for their children and used rewards and punishments to achieve those ends. We do not have the right to impose our values on others, and the approach suggested respects individuals and their right to choose and assists children in developing behavioural patterns which are constructive, satisfying, responsible, and expansive.

When the approaches which now follow are employed, together with encouragement and behavioural consequences, parents should find that their attitudes towards children, frequently characterised by uncertainty, fear, doubt, frustration, and even despair, begin to change to pleasure, confidence, satisfaction, and pride. Attitudes are a product or a consequence of the techniques used. It is not sufficient to have only favourable attitudes towards children. How can you have these attitudes when you are constantly annoyed, provoked, defeated by children? Parents need techniques of raising children, the application of which results in the favourable attitudes described. Every parent can become a better parent by the use of more effective techniques. Some additional approaches which are designed to increase parents' effectiveness are now discussed.

Establish the Family as the Decision-making Body

With the development of democratic patterns, the authority of the adult has weakened and has been replaced by the authority of the group. There is no one person who knows what is right for another or who has the right to enforce compliance. Parents should see that their role now is that of a leader rather than that of a 'boss', a role which will require them to emphasise stimulation from within rather than pressure from without in their relationship with children.

The success of parents depends largely on their ability to integrate or unite the respective members of their families. When this is accomplished, co-operation between members of a family is possible while competition, a condition which denies all children a place in the family through similar activity, is rejected. At present, many families are characterised by competition and lack of unity. Children are compared with others, the successful scholar discourages others from entering that field, misbehaviour abounds because children are made to feel inferior or superior depending on their success as judged by others. Competitive children can stand competition only if they succeed, an unlikely circumstance given today's competitive society.

It is apparent from watching parents that they still feel that they are personally responsible for controlling the behaviour of all children in the family. They deal with each child individually, rewarding and punishing as the occasion arises. They fail to see that the behaviour of each child is influenced by the behaviour of the others and that any corrective effort will fail unless it involves all members of the family. It is not one or two parents who are responsible for three children but a group of four or five which is responsible for all members within the group. The family is much more powerful in influencing behaviour than are parents. Therefore it becomes necessary for parents to learn to use the family to help with the behaviours of children. It is *never* mother's problem, father's problem, Sally's problem, or John's problem; it is *always* our problem, an approach which accepts shared responsibility rather than parental domination.

The author recently gave a family counselling demonstration which involved an 8-year-old boy and a 6-year-old girl. When asked:

'Whose responsibility is it to run a family?', they responded 'Parents'. 'Whose responsibility is it to keep the house?' — 'Mum'. Here is a family, not uncommon, in which the children feel that they have no role to play or no responsibility to assist the family function effectively. There is no cohesion in the family as each member has his or her own territory.

In summary, the group approach would endorse the following:
(a) The authority of the adult has been replaced by the authority of the group.
(b) The family, rather than the parents, is responsible for the behaviour of its members.
(c) Parents are family leaders whose task it is to unite the family for common purposes.
(d) Co-operation is prerequisite for harmonious functioning within the family and can only be achieved in a unified family.

The most effective means for parents to attain a cohesive family, one in which members feel 'This is my family' and are willing to take responsibility in it, is the use of a family council. The family council is a name for a family discussion group which meets regularly to discuss issues which are of concern to the family. The type of issue raised may concern the rules for living together such as: bedtime, household chores, family outings, television viewing, mealtimes, pocket money, family purchases, and general routine matters. The essential point is this: Children need rules but they want a voice in making them.

Consider a typical item raised at a family discussion, bedtime. Mother might raise the question of Sally's bedtime. 'You are now eight, Sally. Last year you went to bed at 7.30 p.m. What do you think would be appropriate for you now that you are a little older?' After some discussion, it is agreed that 8 p.m. would be about right. Do you think that Sally will go to bed when 8 o'clock comes? Of course she will. Children usually accept decisions that they have been involved in making. Contrast this procedure with the traditional home in which a parent arbitrarily decides the bedtimes of children. If mother says: 'You will go to bed at 8, Sally', do you think that Sally is likely to go without constant reminders, threats, and even punishment?

The allocation of responsibilities is another type of item which would be raised at the family council. Children need to have a responsible part in the family life, but it is wise to let them have some choice in the jobs that they should do. The household chores might be listed for the meeting — dishes to be washed, lawns to be cut, rubbish to be removed, and the table to be set. Members of the family then select which ones they are prepared to do. They now know ahead of time what they must do and can plan their time accordingly. If a child fails to meet a commitment, consequences are applied. For example, Jan offers to wash the dishes. On Tuesday, she fails to do so. What is the consequence? Well, there is no point in mother cooking breakfast next morning as there are no clean plates on which to serve it.

Perhaps you think this is unfair to other members of the family. What children must learn is that they function as wheels on a vehicle; if any one wheel doesn't function, the vehicle comes to a halt. In this case, when one child doesn't function, the family comes to a halt. That is a very realistic learning situation for a child and you can be sure that next time a child accepts a responsibility, it will be carried out willingly. We communicate to children that we respect them and depend upon their contribution.

Apart from establishing routines, the other important area which is raised at family council concerns the individual problems of members. All members of the family have the right to raise a problem which they see involving the family. The following is typical: Father raised an incident which occurred on Tuesday. As he drove home from work and went to turn off the busy road into the drive, he found that bicycles and tricycles blocked the drive. He described how he parked illegally in the main street, cleared the drive, got back into his car, drove in, and by the time he was inside he was short-tempered and this spoiled his evening. What could be done about it? Notice that he is not blaming anybody but is concentrating on the needs of the situation, the need to have a clear drive from 6 p.m. onwards.

Mother raised this problem: 'I am annoyed by the continual fighting over television watching. Every night seems to be the same as Bill and Jenny squabble over who is to select each new program. What can we do about it?' After some discussion, it was agreed that the children will alternate, with Jenny selecting the pre-dinner programs on Monday, Bill on Tuesday, and so on. If the procedure did not work out satisfactorily, it would be raised again, at the next family council.

School failure is another area which may be discussed. In a family with two children, Jane, 10, doing very well in school and Nicky 8, doing poorly, father might say to Nicky: 'Would I be right in thinking that you feel you have no chance in the school because Jane is doing so well?' If you observe Nicky for a few seconds, you will observe an imperceptible nod indicating that he is aware of the problem. Then to Jane: 'Would I be right in thinking that you do so well in school in order to be better than Nicky?' Again, a slight nod will be observed after a few seconds, indicating that Jane is also aware of her contribution to Nicky's failure. 'What are you going to do about it, Jane?' responds father. Here is a very important principle. You are your brother's keeper and if any aspect of your behaviour adversely affects others you have a responsibility for doing something about it. Jane might respond: 'Well I have no homework most nights. I will help Nicky with his school work for one hour before dinner on Tuesday and Thursday.' A competitive family in which Nicky cannot succeed scholastically because Jane is doing too well at school is turned into a co-operative family in which each child can be successful in the same area if they wish.

Stealing is a problem which can be resolved only in a family council. Children steal to get even, to revenge, because they feel that they are not liked, are rejected, and do not belong. At a family meeting, mother might raise the question of why Ted feels he has the right to take money out of her purse and from other members of the family. A similar approach would be adopted for a child who damages the toys and possessions of others. The discussion does not centre on the morality of stealing as children know that it is wrong. Rather the purpose of the behaviour is the focus, with questions posed such as: 'Why would somebody want to steal?' 'Would you steal if you wanted to hurt somebody?' 'Would you want to hurt

people who you think dislike you?' 'Could it be that Ted feels that we don't like him?' 'What can we do to show him that we do like him?' Through this type of discussion, children become aware of their goals and can change them. Ted may conclude that he is wrong, that people don't dislike him. Therefore there is no point in trying to hurt them through stealing. The family is the only group which can deal effectively with this type of problem.

'I wonder why it is that Allan feels he has to fight with Shirley so often?' 'I wonder why John feels it necessary to make such negative remarks about Sally's school work?' 'I wonder why we have so much trouble in getting Tim out of bed in the morning?' 'I wonder why we all have to pick up after Sandy?' These are typical problems which are raised at the family meeting although the meeting is not simply a 'gripe' session. One might comment, for instance, 'I want to point out how much easier it is for me to get off to work in the morning now that children are helping to ...'. Recognise the good things that have happened as well as the problems.

The use of the family group will take much of the pressure off the mother. At present mothers have the unenviable position of having to assume too much responsibility for a well-run home. They alone are expected to ensure that jobs are done and have constantly to keep after children to ensure they are up to the mark. Their role is almost that of a policewoman. Tasks such as brushing teeth, washing hands, putting things away, combing hair, completing homework, getting up, catching the school bus, going to bed, eating, and so on, invariably require mother's urging. She should not involve herself in other people's business but may raise these problems at the family discussion or allow the family or child to experience the consequences of the act of neglect.

Conducting a Family Meeting

There are a number of guidelines which have been found to contribute to the effectiveness of the family meeting.

(a) The meeting is held regularly at an agreed time so that individuals can plan to be there.

(b) All members are treated as equals and all have the opportunity to raise problems, make suggestions, and express feelings.

(c) Concentrate on the problem being discussed and, if the discussion is not going well, pinpoint the real issue rather than fall for some other issue such as bickering or arguing.

(d) Decisions made are valid until at least the next family meeting and any complaints by individuals are reserved for the meeting.

(e) Focus on positive aspects of the family and its members as well as the problems and routines.

(f) Decide on the length of the meeting and keep within those limits.

(g) If the family cannot reach consensus on an issue, defer it until the next meeting. Do not decide issues by voting but seek agreement.

(h) At the conclusion of the meeting, summarise decisions and indicate individual responsibilities agreed to.

(i) As family meetings are for the purpose of making decisions about concerns that involve those living together, single parents can conduct meetings as effectively as a two-parent family. The absence of one parent is no deterrent to the successful conduct of a meeting. The benefits flowing from such meetings may soon convince the absent one of the value of the procedure.

One final point. Conversation between parents and their children should be an opportunity to have fun together, to enjoy each other's company and to share experiences. At present, much conversation is of a critical nature in which children are rebuked for their failure to perform chores, preached at by parents for their deficiencies, and so on. The use of the family meeting will minimise this negative approach. If parents or children are unhappy or dissatisfied with any aspect of family living, they raise these matters at the family meeting. At other times, conversation between members of the family is a pleasant activity, free of criticisms and complaints. For example, do not rebuke children at meal-time for any aspect of their eating but reserve that problem for the occasion where it is appropriate — the family meeting.

The family meeting gives children an experience in the democratic way of life and provides valuable experiences in learning to make decisions, take responsibility, and to become aware of the feelings and concerns of others. It is a remarkably uniting experience and brings members of the family closer together as they share the responsibilities of their home and their family.

Communicating with Children

The approach suggested in this book would support parental actions rather than words. 'How many times have I told you' has been said a thousand times by a thousand parents. Children become 'parent deaf' or 'mother deaf' when words are used as the method of control but they will think twice before engaging in unacceptable behaviour if they are going to experience the consequence of that behaviour. For instance, talking with children about the incidence of fighting will not reduce it; urging them to eat will not have the desired effect; reminders about picking up toys will need to be repeated often; discussions about 'bad habits' will have no effect. However, a parent who acts, rather than talks, will impress children with the futility of the above behaviours. A child who is sulking or whining will cease to do so when mother announces: 'I do not want to be with you when you are like that' — and leaves the room. Similar actions are taken when a child swears or engages in behaviours which parents find unacceptable. Recognise the power of our actions and the futility of words.

There are times, however, when it is appropriate to respond verbally to a child's misbehaviour, problem, or situation. This is particularly true when a child has a problem which requires an effective listener so that the child can verbally work through the problem. It is somewhat less important when you have a problem which has been created by a child. In the latter case, action by the parent would be more appropriate although you may want the child to know how you feel about the particular difficulty or problem.

Children who have problems need to talk them through with parents whose role it is to communicate to the children that they understand how the children *feel* and that they are willing to *assist* children in formulating approaches to deal with the problems. A son might say to his mother: 'I wish I could have a dog too. Billy has great fun playing with his.' A mother who has not heard what the child is really expressing might respond: 'Dogs are too much trouble to look after. The answer is No.' This is not helpful to the child and has the effect of terminating the discussion. A mother who understands communication would detect the meaning and respond: 'You feel that you are missing out by not having a dog.' By reflecting the child's feelings, you show the child that you understand him and are willing to assist him in working through the problem to find an acceptable solution.

Consider the following situation. Your daughter bursts into the kitchen and says: 'I am sick of Billy always playing with my toys when I am out.' An uncommunicative mother might respond: 'Well, I have seen you play with Billy's things without asking him.' A communicative mother might respond: 'I see that you are angry that Billy has played with your toys.' The former terminates the discussion or turns it into a conflict; the latter indicates that she has understood the message and is willing to seek solutions to the problem which has created the anger.

There are times when children's behaviour causes you to have a problem and you would like to raise it with them. In these cases, you may want to let the child know how you feel about the behaviour rather than express your anger, annoyance, or disappointment. For instance, you have run out of milk and need some for dinner. Tim agrees to run to the shop quickly and buy some. He is gone, not five minutes, but for half an hour, having met with friends and decided to play football. A parent fails to communicate who resorts to criticism or punishment. 'That is the last time I ask you to do something. Just forget about going to the football on Saturday.' A parent who wishes to communicate with Tim might say: 'When you don't do what you promise, I get angry because I cannot get the dinner.' This approach will have more influence on the child to behave responsibly than will the punitive approach which will produce 'parent-deaf' children or create power situations.

A girl who has permission to attend an evening concert and to be home by 11 o'clock creates a problem when she fails to return until midnight. An ineffective technique of communication would resort to criticism and punishment. 'Where do you think you have been? I am not going to put up with this. That is the last concert you attend.' A parent who wishes to influence the child would remark: 'When you don't come home when you agreed, I become worried, because I do not know where you are.' There is no blame associated with this form of communication but the parent wants the girl to know that her behaviour has caused the parent considerable worry.

There is a choice to be made in all cases of unsatisfactory behaviour. If a child indicates that he or she has a particular problem, a parent should attempt to reflect the concern expressed by the child, keep the conversation going, and help the child seek possible solutions to the problem. If the child's behaviour has caused the parent to have a problem, the parent can use behavioural consequences or can tell the child how the parent feels about the behaviour. A child who does not get up on time in the morning can either experience the behavioural consequences at school or may be told by a parent: 'When you don't get up in time, I get annoyed, because I have to rush through things to get you off to school.'

A sensitive parent will become aware of those situations in which a child who has a problem needs to express feelings and concerns so that a solution may be arrived at. There are those times, too, when a child creates a problem for a parent who then has the need to express concern or to behave accordingly. The ability to communicate with children is an essential aspect of a democratic home.

Respect Children's Right to Decide

Our homes have traditionally provided an orderly situation for children but have denied them freedom. Parents made almost all decisions for children with respect to such matters as eating, getting dressed, bedtime, television viewing, friendships, speech, chores, and the like. With a shift to a more democratic pattern, parents sought to become more democratic simply by being non-authoritarian. As a consequence, children did as they liked and parents looked in bewilderment at the product of 'democracy'. There can be no freedom without order, but order without freedom is equally damaging.

The situation for which we strive is freedom with order and a pattern of relationships in which respect for each other is the central theme. Parents show no respect for their children when they indulge, spoil, overprotect, dominate, or reject them. Children show no respect for their parents when they subject them to unreasonable demands or when they expect them to accept the responsibility for behaviours which rightly reside with the children.

What is the meaning of respect? You communicate respect when you do not attempt to impose your values upon others. Traditionally, parents have dominated their children in the sense that parents made all decisions for a child. For example, a mother who demands of a child the following: 'Get into that room and tidy it up' or 'Go to the toilet right now' or 'Take that thumb out of your mouth' or 'Off to bed right now' shows no respect for that child. This is the old traditional approach which assumes that parents know what is best for their children and have the right to make the children accept their decision.

In contrast, parents who respect children will not impose their values upon them but will treat them with firmness. Instead of telling children what they must do, parents may tell children what they themselves intend doing. For example, there is no respect in the autocratic demand of a mother to her son: 'Get out of here and wash those hands.' There is respect, however, when mother shows firmness and states: 'I will only serve people with clean hands.' What is she making the child do? Nothing. It is up to the child. If he wants to wash, well and good. If he doesn't want to wash, nothing is said as he experiences the consequences. We are not making him do anything; the choice is with the child.

Many problems in a family stem directly from the attempt by parents to dominate their children. 'Stop that sniffing, eat your beans, pick that up, put that away, get up, go to bed, turn that off, be quiet, stop that, etc., etc.' This is exactly what so many children are fighting today — the authoritative demands of parents.

We must learn to respect children's right to choose but ensure that they experience the consequence of their choice. If they choose not to eat their vegetables, they are given no sweets because they are not hungry. If they choose to lie in, they experience their lateness at school. If they choose to fight, there is no interference from a parent. If they choose to mistreat a hi-fi set, they are removed from the hi-fi room. If we adopt this strategy, children will develop appropriate ways of behaving, not because we have forced them on our children but because they have experienced the consequences of alternate patterns of behaviour.

Don't Be too Concerned with Problem Behaviour

Parents find far too many things to be concerned with in their children. They watch them constantly, noting any aspects of behaviour which need correction. It is almost as if they believe that their children will continue their deficient behaviour unless they are corrected. Such an approach is extremely discouraging to children who interpret their parents' constant correction as a lack of faith in their ability to function effectively.

Why do you correct children who speak incorrectly, walk poorly, eat sloppily, spell badly, or behave unacceptably? Because you believe that children will not rid themselves of these deficiencies unless you correct them. Children make mistakes or behave badly because they either lack skill or because they want to keep you involved with them. In either case, your correction is detrimental to their improvement. If the child lacks skill, your correction will discourage further practice; if it is purposeful, you simply strengthen the deficiency.

Parents should show more confidence in their children and communicate this confidence. Children do have the capacity to work out their own problems in their own way. This suggestion is particularly relevant in the following three areas.

Interpersonal Conflict

The way in which individuals get along together is their business. If your child is having a difficult time with another child, then the faulty relationship existing between the two is their problem, not yours. They have to learn to sort it out in their way. However, if you interfere to 'correct' the situation, what you teach the child is to look to you to sort out all problems.

Similarly, a child who complains about being unfairly treated by a teacher should not expect a parent to go to the school in an attempt to re-train a teacher. Parents should always remain neutral in disputes which do not involve them directly and help their children to see how they may be contributing to a faulty relationship and to consider what they can do about improving it.

Often a dispute between a parent and a child will cause the other parent to become involved. This is inadvisable. If a father smacks a child and the child approaches mother with a complaint about his treatment, mother should not become inolved. A faulty relationship exists between the father and the child and it is their business to sort it out. She might remark, 'I am sorry that you were smacked but I am sure that you will soon learn to get on well with Daddy.' She puts the responsibility where it belongs, with the parties concerned.

Children have to learn to deal with unpleasant people such as a bully, a thief, a tell-tale, a cruel child, or a liar. Further, they have to learn to restore unpleasant situations. There is no need for you to become involved in their problems or to try to shelter them from unpleasantness. These are real situations which children will encounter frequently and they must learn ways of resolving them. Your participation is not only unnecessary but also damaging, for it communicates to the child that, without you, they are not capable of looking after themselves. Remind yourselves frequently that children do have the ability to solve their own problems and that, by listening carefully to what they say, by helping them explore solutions, we assist them to cope with interpersonal conflicts, conflicts which will always exist and which need to be resolved in an atmosphere of mutual respect and co-operation.

Encourage Independence

Children will move through various stages from complete dependence to considerable independence if they are encouraged to do so.

For some children, this gradual acquisition of independence is frustrated or denied by parents who continue to do things that children are capable of doing for themselves. Many parents teach their children this message: 'I don't need to take care of myself. That's mother's (or father's) job.'

Routine tasks which must be learned include feeding oneself, dressing, personal hygiene, and caring for possessions. It is the child's responsibility to learn these tasks, and provided parents offer sufficient training and encouragement, there is no need for parents to perform these routines for their children. Never do for children what they can do for themselves. When we accept children's responsibilities, we put ourselves into their service, hinder the development of independence, and deprive children of the opportunities for learning from realistic situations.

If requested by your five-year-old to help put on his coat, a parent might reply, 'I am sure that you can manage that yourself'. To a child who requests help with picking up his toys, raking up lawn clippings, or brushing a dog, a similar reply would be appropriate. This is not to suggest that we reject genuine requests for assistance when a child lacks the necessary skill or strength for a task, but we do not involve ourselves in those tasks which belong to the child and those which he or she is capable of performing. Stimulate independence by providing opportunities for your children and then acknowledge their performance with a 'well done' gesture.

Don't Be Impressed by Bad Habits

Another area requiring a display of parental confidence in their children is that which relates to bad habits. Parents should exercise considerable restraint and exhibit genuine unconcern with these behaviours. Activities such as thumb sucking, nail biting, nose picking,

masturbation, and swearing worry parents and they often feel obliged to do something about them. When children observe that their parents are concerned with these particular behaviours, it is likely that they will be well cultivated by children who now know that they have a strong weapon with which to defeat parents.

Do not be concerned with these 'bad habits'. Attribute little importance to them. Do not be impressed by a child who swears or lies, and keep your reaction at low key. Take a long-range view of these behaviours. Remember the child who concerned you greatly two years ago with his bedwetting? 'Why did we worry so much about him, I wonder?' This is the typical situation. A child who is thumb sucking or nail biting will not be doing those things next year or the year after. If you are genuinely unconcerned, you will find that the behaviours disappear more quickly as the child sees that you have no stake in them. By communicating to children our unconcern with the behaviour and our faith in their ability to cope with it, we eradicate inappropriate behaviours which otherwise may be thoroughly cultivated.

Help Children Identify Their Mistaken Goals

There is no value in asking a child the following types of questions: 'Why did you keep annoying me?' 'Why won't you do what I tell you?' 'Why don't you go to bed when I tell you?' The only honest answer is 'I don't know'. If children were aware of their goals, they could change them without help from others. They tend not to change because they are unaware of the purposes of their behaviour.

Parents can help children become aware of their goals by the following procedure. John keeps losing things and his parents have to keep replacing them when they cannot be found. At a family meeting, a parent might say: 'John, would I be right in thinking that the reason you lose things is to keep Mum and Dad looking for them?' John will think that remark over for a few seconds before his facial expression will change and his eyes will smile and a sheepish grin will appear, indicating that parents have accurately guessed the purpose behind losing things.

Parents can determine the child's purpose quite easily. To keep people busy, to demonstrate power, to hurt or to show inadequacy. Children are not aware of their purposes and have no idea as to why they behave in certain ways. We can 'shock' them into recognition of the goal through this indirect exposure. 'Mary, your parents tell me that they cannot get you off to bed at night time. Is that right?' 'Yes.' 'Could it be, Mary, that you do not go to bed because you want to show your parents that you can do just what you want and not what they want?' The resultant smile is a clear indication of the correctness of the interpretation and now opens the possibility of changing the behaviour.

Try these

(1) Which mother is displaying firmness?
   (a) 'Get into that room and finish your piano lesson.'
   (b) 'I will only pay for music lessons if you are going to practise.'

(2) Which mother is displaying respect?
   (a) 'I can only take people shopping who are neatly dressed.'
   (b) 'Take that dirty shirt off before you come shopping with me.'

(3) Which mother is using firmness?
   (a) 'If you don't take that thumb out of your mouth, your teeth will start to grow out.'
   (b) 'I don't wish to hold your hand if it has been in your mouth.'

(4) Father has agreed to maintain the house and the garden; mother has agreed to provide clean clothes and all meals. Mother decides that John will sweep the yard and Tim will do the dishes. On Tuesday night, Tim does not do the dishes. Mother demands more co-operation from the children.
   What mistakes does she make?

(5) Which parent is communicating more effectively to a child who is crying because of a broken toy?
   (a) 'You will just have to take better care of your toys.'
   (b) 'I see that you are very upset over your broken toy.'

(6) Which parent encourages a child to be more responsible?
   (a) 'When you don't come home from school on time I get worried, because I don't know where you are.'
   (b) 'I am sick of your coming home late from school. You can miss TV tonight.'

(7) Which parent is using the family discussion session well?

    (a) 'I have listened to the discussion and have decided that we do not need a colour TV set.'

    (b) 'It seems to me that we are not ready to come to a decision on buying a colour TV set.'

Answers

(1) (b)

(2) (a)

(3) (b)

(4) (i) Tasks to be performed by children should be decided at the family meeting, not by mother.

    (ii) The notion of co-operation as used by mother is 'Do what I tell you to do.'

    (iii) Mother should not comment on the dishes being unwashed but she should not cook breakfast next morning.

(5) (b)

(6) (a)

(7) (b)

8
Adolescence

Why the Problem?

While adolescence has generally been considered a difficult period, today's teenagers seem more troubled than those of previous generations. Concern is increasing as the percentage of young people involved in aberrant or illicit behaviour grows. Statistics on drugs, alcohol and substance abuse, juvenile crime, suicide and sexual activity indicate an increase in the frequency and numbers of individuals involved.

Young people today have grown up during a period of affluence where even the poor have been cushioned against severe poverty. Electronic media, computers and automobiles are commonplace to them. They were also born and raised during a period of great social and political upheaval which included the Vietnam war, the 1960s youth revolt, soaring crime rates, high-technology revolution, the arms race, runaway inflation, rapidly rising divorce rates, two-income families, sexual revolution, overt homosexuality, women's liberation, black power and terrorism. All have helped shape juvenile behaviour and are factors which are related to the problems which parents experience in relation to their adolescents.

A chapter on adolescent behaviour has been requested by a variety of sources including parents, teachers, youth and social workers and community welfare staff. Parents find the adolescent period particularly confusing when previously pleasant children begin to display unco-operative, aggressive and provocative behaviour. The mask of childhood is dropped as adolescents begin to exercise their newly acquired independence and it is during this period that the effectiveness of parents will be clearly demonstrated. Be sure of one thing: parent education and sensible upbringing will minimise or prevent serious problems arising during adolescence. There is nothing inevitable about the myth of the 'storm and stress' of adolescence and there is no young person who cannot be helped by parents who have established sound relationships with their children during childhood.

It is important to note that the principles which are discussed in relation to adolescence are no different from those which are appropriate to individuals of all ages. Probably the most important difference in adolescence compared with childhood is the increasing degree of autonomy and independence which teenagers experience. What does not change, however, is the need to establish and maintain relationships between parents and adolescents which are based on equality, mutual respect and trust. Without such relationships, parents can abandon hope that adolescence will be anything other than a war between the two generations.

The particular problems which parents may face during adolescence involve alcohol, drugs, cars, sex, stealing, delinquency, violence and defiance. As indicated earlier, all are appropriately grouped under the four goals of attention, power, revenge or withdrawal. In adolescence, the goals of power and revenge begin to dominate and replace the attention-seeking behaviours which are characteristic of younger children. As Dreikurs (1968:29) observes:

> The battle between parents and children for power and domination may reach a point where the parents try every conceivable means to subjugate the culprits. The mutual antagonism may become so strong that each party has only one desire: retaliation, to revenge his own feeling of being hurt.

Delinquency is now a major problem in most countries. Its origins, however, like most other difficult behaviours, are found in the mistakes which parents make during the formative years. All failures in adolescence reveal themselves as former problem children — children who did not adjust themselves in co-operating as an equal member within the family. If parents have used the techniques of encouragement, consequences and family meetings, and have established relationships based on equality and respect, adolescence will hold no fears. The answer to delinquency, drugs, alcohol and the like is prevention. As Manaster and Corsini (1982:96) correctly observe:

> Every delinquent starts in the home: children only attack others if they have been trained to attack in the family. Parents who are either brutal or neglectful or spoiling are equally liable to generate delinquents through their misguided methods of dealing with their young ones . . .

Better parenting is the major solution we recommend to counteract delinquency.

Typical Parental Errors in Adolescence

In dealing with adolescents, parents typically make two types of mistakes. One is to assume that adolescence is a stage through which all individuals pass and that unacceptable behaviour is a temporary phenomenon which will disappear as their young adolescent becomes more mature. This permissive approach is reflected in the attitude of simply weathering the storm. The other mistake is to view the increasing independence of the adolescent as a threat which must be dealt with by increasing parental control and domination. In their desire to be seen as responsible parents with responsible children, any deviation in adolescent behaviour such as substance abuse, school failure or extremes of dress, must be dealt with swiftly, firmly and with authority.

Permissive Parenting

To view adolescence as a period which is inevitably rebellious during which parents have little potential to influence their teenagers is to accept and condone irresponsibility in their youngsters. Permissive parents act to avoid conflict as they see themselves as powerless to influence their teenagers. As a result, they tolerate activities such as alcohol abuse, drug taking, sexual promiscuity, disrespect for authority, property and the rights of others, vandalism and offensive behaviour. The adolescent interprets this permissive approach as an open invitation to do as they wish.

When parents allow freedom without order, they lose respect in the eyes of their children who see them as weak, unable to provide guidance and incapable of maintaining the cohesiveness of the family. Further, adolescents who are subject to permissive parents, begin to lose respect for themselves as they sense their parents have given up hope for them, do not value them and are simply waiting until their teenagers are old enough to leave the home.

Autocratic Parenting

While permissiveness is an ineffective method of influencing adolescents, the hardening of parental attitudes and approaches to adolescents is equally damaging. This coercive approach is supported by certain irrational beliefs by parents, chief of which is that parents are responsible for the behaviour of their children and that if they were more effective as parents, the adolescents would always be well behaved. Such parents believe that teenagers should turn out the way parents want them to be and it is the parents' task to impose beliefs, values, behaviours, and standards on their adolescents.

When parents attempt to force their teenagers to behave in certain ways, the youngsters will react in one of two ways. They will become discouraged, believing that they are unable to cope with the problems of living or they will become rebellious and refuse to accept any parental suggestion. Parents who use coercive approaches may have initial success during the pre-adolescent years as they are able to force conformity on the younger child. However, adolescents learn that they have the power to withhold co-operation from parents and begin to exercise that power in matters such as smoking, schooling, choice of friends, sex, alcohol, TV viewing and leisure activities. The increased efforts by parents to control their adolescents through coercive methods only serve to invite further resistance and withdrawal of co-operation by the adolescent.

The following activities are examples of each of the following types of parent.

Permissive Parent	Coercive Parent
Drives son to school although bus available	Criticises son's school work
Tidies daughter's room and makes bed	Finds faults with daughter's friends
Is not aware of where son is in the evenings	Uses physical punishment
Prepares meals for daughter on request	Tolerates no disagreement with parent's views
Allows unlimited TV viewing	Demands that son does homework
Sets no guidelines re alcohol consumption	

It has been suggested throughout this book that all problems which parents encounter with children and adolescents originate from a faulty relationship. How problems are handled during the teens is dependent upon the relationship existing between parents and their teenagers. Mutual respect and trust form the basis for a relationship based upon equality, the only type of relationship which is effective in today's society. The characteristics of a relationship based on equality have been described by Dinkmeyer and McKay (1983:7) as

- Mutual concern and caring
- Empathy for one another
- A desire to listen to one another
- Emphasis on assets rather than faults
- A commitment to co-operative and equal participation in resolving conflicts
- Sharing of thoughts and feelings rather than hiding them and bearing resentment
- Mutual commitment to common goals
- Support for and acceptance of one another — as imperfect people in the process of growing.

Previous chapters have indicated a framework for understanding human behaviour and while this framework is equally applicable to adolescents, there are a number of aspects which are particularly relevant to the adolescent.

It is the author's experience when working with adolescents who are regarded as having behavioural problems that they share certain common characteristics. These are:

1 They view themselves as failures in life.
2 They are pessimistic about the future.
3 They lack the courage to take a chance.
4 They have been humiliated frequently.

The Possibility of Change

These faulty views and their correction is the basis of helping the troubled adolescent. It is essential to realise that 'everything can be something else', that anything is possible, that adolescents are not victims of upbringing, of heredity, of emotion, of schooling or of society. They do not drink excessively because of parental neglect or lack of supervision. They decide on the way in which they will behave and contribute very much to their own lives; they are not victims of circumstance or passive objects in the game of life. 'Individuals are responsible for their behaviour. One has considerable control over one's life.' (Manaster and Corsini, 1982:161) It is essential to recognise the potential of any individual to change immediately. Think through the implications of the following question: 'Could David behave well if his life depended on it?' The answer is always

'Yes', indicating that life can always be modified by an individual changing his viewpoint, decision, belief or judgment. The adolescent is always responsible.

While children are small, conflict with adults is confined to home and to school. During adolescence, the conflict is directed against society as a whole and all members of society suffer as a result of their inability to influence teenagers.

A basic principle involves the adolescent's need to feel a sense of belonging, of being part of, of being integrated into the community, to be recognised and appreciated by others. However, the competitive society in which we live encourages parents to instil high ambition and achievement into their children, to be the best, to be superior. Consequently, many young people are denied the opportunity to feel important through useful accomplishments. For each teenager who achieves significance through scholastic, social or athletic success, many thousands find no such opportunity. As a result they turn to behaviours which are admired by their peers but rejected by adults. These include smoking, taking drugs, driving wildly, making easy money, indulgence in sexual activity, stealing or vandalism — all such acts lend themselves to obtaining a sense of importance.

Make no mistake, adolescents are looking for guidance, for advice or help, but they find so few adults who will treat them as equals. The more the troubled adolescent needs help and guidance, the more they are punished, threatened, lectured to, admonished, discriminated against and made to feel inferior and worthless. Nothing will

be effective with teenagers until parents, teachers and others who deal with youth are prepared to change their own behaviour and begin to establish more effective relationships with young people. Such changes will include:

1. *Change your own behaviour rather than the adolescent's behaviour*

Parents who try to change the behaviour of adolescents will invariably fail. Parents are naturally concerned about such behaviours as defiance, stealing, lying, violence, alcohol and drug abuse, school failure or drop-out, rudeness, neglect of responsibility and disobedience. Faced with such behaviours, parents usually resort to punitive methods in an attempt to change the adolescent. As a result, relationships suffer, hostility is generated, retaliation invited and no final victory is achieved by either parent or adolescent.

Probably the most powerful message coming from modern psychology is this: 'If you wish to change the behaviour of another person, change your own behaviour first.' Parents are always full of good intentions provided that their adolescent is prepared to change. As long as parents are convinced about what their sons or daughters should do, what the other spouse should do, or what teachers should do, they will overlook the only influence which they can be using to resolve conflict — themselves.

While parents are greatly interested in learning about approaches whereby they can change their children's behaviour, they generally fail to realise that children will change only when parents are prepared to change. As Dreikurs (1972:205) pointed out:

> We all try to change the other one and have no luck. Stop thinking about what the other one should do; the only one we can change is ourselves.

As applied to the goals of misbehaviour which were discussed in Chapter 3, the above suggestion would result in the following parental reactions to typical adolescent behaviours.

Behaviour	Goals of Behaviour	Parental Response
Neglecting chores Clowning Minor mischief Unusual dressing	Attention seeking	1 Refuse to give special attention on request. 2 Look for opportunities to comment for useful contribution. 3 Allow consequences to take place.
Drug-taking Disobedience Hostility Stubbornness Apathy	Power	1 Refuse to fight. 2 Admit that you cannot make son/daughter do anything. 3 Allow consequences to follow.

Stealing	Revenge	1 Refuse to be hurt.
Delinquency		2 Avoid retaliation.
Rudeness		3 Work to establish better
Violence		relationship.
		4 Maintain order.
Giving up easily	Withdrawal	1 Avoid criticism.
Failing in school		2 Look for slight improvement.
Truancy		3 Acknowledge effort.
Excessive TV watching		4 Never give up.

In summary, a challenge to parents in raising adolescents is to change themselves rather than their teenagers. Recognise that we cannot make another person do anything and that, in the final analysis, the only person for whom we are totally responsible is ourselves. When we stop thinking about what others should do, and focus on what we can do, the power to influence others becomes enormous.

2 Encouragement

Many parents of teenagers report that their children lack motivation for school learning, are not interested in sport, and are generally apathetic about much of life. These young people are of great concern to parents who begin to doubt their own effectiveness as parents and begin to despair about their children's futures.

Behind all difficult adolescents there are discouraged individuals who believe that they have no chance of being successful or of making progress, who lack self-confidence, who are pessimistic about the future, who refuse to take risks and who have low opinions of themselves. Rarely has the author encountered an adolescent with major problems who does not possess the above characteristics. The modification of these faulty views held by adolescents is the basis for all corrective work and the heart of such correction in the encouragement process.

Chapter 6 has discussed the nature of encouragement and the techniques of application. The process of encouragement is just so basic that it must be thoroughly understood and applied. Failure to do so underlies so much of our difficulties with individuals. It is so common when one talks with adolescents who are having difficulty at home, at school or in society, to hear them describe their life as a series of discouraging experiences. Parents are the prime source of discouragement although their intentions are otherwise. Life for the adolescent in such circumstances is the expectation of failure, a hypothesis which becomes self-fulfilling. The ability to encourage is the most important single quality in establishing effective relationships with adolescents.

The sources of discouragement during adolescence which involve parents include over-ambition, negative expectations, peer comparison, concern with prestige or status, mistake centred approaches, and conditional acceptance. Statements which reflect the above are:

'Come on John, you can do better.'

'I think that two mathematics would be too much for you.'

'Why don't you study hard like your brother?'

'You will have to work harder to lift those grades.'

'There is no excuse for these poor marks.'

'I see that you are still having trouble with English.'

'I expect you have been up to something, David.'

'What will others think of us if you are dressed like that?'

'Well, I am not prepared to have a failure in this family.'

'If you improve your manners, I will think about a bicycle for you.'

'You will never amount to anything with those attitudes.'

Methods of encouraging adolescents are similar to those employed in encouraging people of all ages. They are concerned with:

1 Focus on assets and strengths while minimising mistakes.

2 Acknowledgment of effort, improvement and contributions.

3 Communication of confidence in teenagers' ability to manage their own affairs.

4 Comments on processes not products, acts not actors.

The following examples demonstrate the application of the above principles:

1 'I see that your backhand is now much stronger.'
2 'Thanks for cleaning the car. It certainly makes my work easier.'
3 'It does take a lot of effort to plan your subjects. But knowing you, I am sure that you will do a good job.'
4 'I see from your school report that you have put a lot of work into science this term.'

In summary, to encourage your teenagers is to convey to them that you have faith in them as they are now and in their ability to handle future problems. When adolescents know that their parents have confidence in them, they can develop confidence in themselves.

3 Independence, Responsibility and Discipline

Adolescence is a time of increased independence coupled with increased responsibility. As many parents have learned to their sorrow, to grant one without the other is to court disaster. While there is a clear need for more independence in matters such as leisure activities, bed-time, scholastic decisions, occupational choice, friendship, dating and the like, each independent choice made by the adolescent will produce a consequence which the adolescent must experience. This series of events — choice, decisions and consequences, is the basis for teaching adolescents to accept responsibilities, to be self-disciplined.

To help adolescents to become responsible for their own behaviour, parents must free themselves of the notion that they are personally responsible for the behaviour of their teenagers. The strong desire to be a 'good parent', to be a 'responsible parent', often results in parents attempting to maintain their traditional authority over children by tightening up, by exerting greater pressure, practices which are bound to invite rebellion and resistance. This is particularly common in relation to school achievement where the author has had the experience of dealing with so many under-achieving students whose lack of success is the direct result of parental intervention or pressure on the students to 'achieve', to 'excel'.

It is essential for parents who wish to produce responsible young individuals, that they identify in those areas of responsibility where a particular problem is located, that they permit the appropriate individual to choose, and the consequences resulting from this decision are experienced by the individual. If you fail to pay the gas-bill, what happens? Arrive late at the airport? Overeat? Run a red traffic light?

This is the way life is and from these experiences we learn one thing
— to be responsible for our own behaviour.

Traditionally parents have used rewards and punishments in an
attempt to teach their adolescents to behave responsibly. Apart from
violating the values of mutual respect and equality, these approaches
are ineffective today. Adolescents who are punished, criticised,
denied privileges, or threatened will simply retaliate in kind. The
resultant relationship between parents and their adolescents is
characterised by rebellion and hostility. Adolescents are autonomous
people and we cannot make them do anything.

Rewards are similarly ineffective in teaching adolescents to be
responsible. Rewards communicate a clear message: 'Never do anything for nothing.' Teenagers have a strong desire to contribute to
family living and parents should capitalise on this desire rather than
destroy it by offering rewards in order to secure a contribution. A
parent recently asked me the question: 'I have promised my lad an
overseas trip if he passes his Higher School Certificate. Have I done
the wrong thing?' What do you think?

As suggested in Chapter 6, an alternative to reward and punishment is to allow teenagers to experience the consequences of their
own behaviour. A student who fails to complete homework, will
experience the consequence at school. Clothes not put in the dirty
linen basket will not be washed. The car left unwashed will not be
available for a period of time. This is the basis of self-discipline. It
respects the adolescents' right to decide and holds them responsible
for their decisions.

Parents will frequently need to negotiate consequences with their
teenagers. Consider a 15-year-old girl who wishes to go skating on
Friday evenings. After some discussion, it is agreed between the girl
and her parents that midnight would be a reasonable hour for the
girl to be home. On one particular evening, she arrives home at 1.30
a.m. Nothing is said by the parent at that time but on the following
morning a parent might say to the girl: 'I see you are not yet able
to keep to your agreement. Ask about skating again in two weeks'
time.'

The above procedure highlights a number of points:

1 A choice is presented. Either be home by the agreed-upon time
  or miss skating for two weeks.
2 Parents follow through. Consequences must be experienced or
  the girl learns that agreements matter for nought.
3 Behaviours and consequences are negotiated. Adolescents are

more likely to accept a decision if they have been involved in making it.

4 Conflict is avoided. Nothing is said to the girl at the time the agreement is violated but parents wait until both they and the adolescent are calm and refrain from discussing the matter when the 'heat' is on.

The aim of the above procedure, utilising logical consequences, is to assist young people to become responsible. It could be applied to use of the family car, organisation of parties, alcohol consumption and the like. It is an approach which respects young people, treats them as social equals, develops a co-operative working relationship, and balances independence with responsibility.

4 Shared Responsibility

It is necessary to recognise that adolescents are rapidly becoming autonomous individuals. Whereas the younger child is far more dependent upon parents, the adolescent today is capable of deciding and acting independently of parents. Indeed, the peer group is a far more influential factor in the adolescent's life than is the parent's influence. Today, given the increase in divorce, the growth of two-income families, and the surge of single-parent families, adolescents are more at the mercy of peer pressure than they were a decade or so ago. It is necessary, therefore, to win adolescent co-operation by involving them in decisions which concern them. Failure to do so will frequently result in the adolescent failing to co-operate with the decisions made by the parents. While parents may force a young child to behave as they wish, their success with adolescence will be minimal. Indeed, it usually has the opposite effect. A parent who demands: 'You be home by 11 o'clock' can expect the adolescent some time after midnight. The demand: 'There will be no smoking in this house' is to invite the behaviour despite the adolescent's reluctance. Telling adolescents what they must or must not do is to invite defeat. However, when they are included in such matters as chores, homework, maintaining their room, use of the family car, purchase of their own clothes, family problems, and allowances, teenagers feel that they are equal members of the family, respected and trusted, and have ideas and suggestions which people value. These beliefs greatly contribute to the establishment of good relationships between parents and adolescents, the basis for parenting with teenage children.

Try these

(1) Consider the following practices. Classify them according to the criterion of:
   (a) Which parent pampers the teenager?
   (b) Which parent is coercive?
   (c) Which parent encourages the teenager?

   1 Parents are intimidated by teenager who threatens to leave home and are reluctant to say 'no' to his/her requests.
   2 Parents use the family meeting as the basic approach to solving problems.
   3 Parents consistently criticise the way in which the teenager keeps his room.
   4 Parents invite teenagers to contribute opinions on family problems.
   5 Teenager eats her dinner in front of television instead of with family.
   6 Parents make disparaging remarks about their daughter's friends.

(2) The following extract is from an Australian newspaper report (the Northern Territory *News*, 4.3.1985):

   'The stability of a 15-year-old girl's home environment must be questioned when she was out on the streets at midnight and drunk,' the Chief Magistrate said in the Juvenile Court.

   (a) Does the Chief Magistrate believe that individuals are responsible for their own behaviour?
   (b) Can parents prevent a 15-year-old girl from going out at night and from drinking?
   (c) Who is responsible for the girl's behaviour?
   (d) What can be done to help the girl become more responsible?

Answers

(1) (a) Pampering 1; 5
   (b) Coercive 3; 6
   (c) Encouraging 2; 4

(2) (a) No, the parents are held to be responsible.
   (b) No, the young lady is autonomous.

(c) The young girl; all individuals are in charge of their own behaviour.

(d) Parents could reach an agreement with the girl about times of returning home and drinking. If agreement is broken, parents follow through with the consequences agreed to.

9

Single-parent Families

There are a number of categories of parents with special problems in relation to children. They are divorced parents, never-married parents, widowed parents, adopting parents and step-parents. Although the basic principles discussed in this book apply to all types of situations, the above families usually experience some special problems which will be discussed in this chapter.

Basic Principles for all Single-parent Families

For all types of single-parent families there are some specific techniques which are appropriate to all. Baruth (1979) has suggested the following:

  1 Be honest with your children about the situation that caused you to become a single parent. This should only be done to the extent that the children can understand and every effort should be made

to present your spouse in a favourable light. Nothing is to be gained by making disparaging remarks about your former spouse.

2 If the situation involves a separation or divorce, assure the children that they are not responsible for the decision to discontinue the relationship.

3 Be honest about your own feelings. This will demonstrate to the children that it is all right for them to express how they feel. It is important, however, that after feelings have been expressed that constructive action be taken to begin coping with the situation. You should realise that feelings of anger, anxiety, and fear are frequent reactions to the situation. However, if such feelings persist for an extended period of time, professional help should be sought.

4 Try to maintain as much of the same routine and surroundings as possible. This will provide the children with a feeling of security that not everything has changed.

5 Do not try to be both mother and father to your children. Establish a family atmosphere of team work where responsibilities are shared.

6 In the case of separation or divorce, realise that the relationship is over and do not encourage the children to hope for a reconciliation.

7 The children must be reassured that they will continue to be loved, cared for, and supported. This should be done not only by words but also by your attitude and behaviour.

8 You should not use the children in an effort to gain bargaining power with your separated or divorced spouse. Differences should be settled privately between the parents or in court.

9 Make use of grandparents and other relatives so the children maintain a sense of belonging to a continuing family.

10 Try to seek the companionship and counsel of other single parents.

There are many sources of advice and support that will help immeasurably in child rearing. Many churches and communities have organisations for the single parent.

The families to be discussed in this chapter are referred to as single-parent families and collectively they form a large part of our society. While the problems initially faced by single parents are often related to the event which led to their current status, their problems become more similar not only to other single-parent families but to two-parent families as well. The special problem which single parents face initially will now be discussed.

Divorced Parents

As with any single-parent family, the event which leads to the uniqueness of the family requires a great deal of emotional and social adjustment. Unlike the death of a spouse, divorce does not occur suddenly and it is possible for parents to prepare their children for a life in a one-parent family.

If parents who are contemplating divorce would seek counselling before rather than after separation, they would have far fewer problems with their children. Children do not think that their parents will separate even though they witness fighting and arguments. It comes as a shock to them to be told of the separation and they become angry, frustrated, guilty and ambivalent, emotions which will also be felt by the single parents. Adequate preparation for the separation will lessen the intensity of these emotions in children.

A question frequently asked is this: 'What is better for the child. To have two parents who do not get on well or to be raised by a single-parent family?' It is not possible to say that one is better than the other. Many children suffer when parents do not get along well yet they will not say anything. They internalise their anger and fear but they will express those emotions to a marriage counsellor. Children worry about possible physical harm to one parent, or they feel sorry for one. The less parents quarrel, the less they abuse each other, the better it is for children. Parents who are considering divorce should have discussions with each other which are not ugly; if that is impossible, discussions should be held when the children are not about.

Children have a strong need to be proud of their parents who are, after all, the foundation of their lives. Therefore, it is very hurtful to hear parents saying unpleasant things about each other no matter how true they may be. Parents are seen by their children as being very special and it only creates distance between a parent and a child when one parent is disrespectful to the other. 'Your father has money but he won't buy you clothes.' 'Your mother is lazy and does not have meals ready.' Such statements, before or after separation, are unnecessary and hurtful. They will result in parents losing their own cause as their criticism of their spouse will result in their losing the respect of their children.

Children have to be helped to realise, when separation is being considered, that their parents have a problem as a *couple* but that does not affect them as human beings or lessen the respect of children for them. Indeed, it is an opportunity for a child to show respect by being helpful in the separation. Children realise that the parental difficulties are creating unhappiness in their parents and that this unhappiness is increased when children turn against them. Children can assist by not making demands, by not abusing parents or by not protecting one parent from the other. Children must be helped to confront the reality of the separation but with an attitude of: 'What can I do to be helpful?' This is another example of a principle discussed earlier. Our behaviour reflects our decisions and children in a separating family can choose to be difficult or to be helpful. The separation in itself causes nothing in terms of behaviour but is the opportunity for a variety of behaviours.

In preparing children for separation, the best individuals to counsel the children are the parents. However, if there is too much anger between them, too much crying or too much fighting, then another person should be sought.

Following the separation, a particular problem which arises concerns visiting rights. Children may not wish to visit a particular parent when that parent tries to undermine the other through action or words. A mother should not attempt to control the relationship between children and their father and vice versa. Relationships belong to the people involved. When children are torn, as they frequently are, it is better to be respectful, acknowledge the children's problem and try to teach children better techniques for dealing with a parent who wants to deprecate the other. There are many things in life which we cannot control and the behaviour of a spouse is one. On the other hand, children should not receive special service from either parent when they appear to be 'torn' by the conflicting information which they are receiving from each parent.

One final point about separation. When one parent is over-responsive, somebody else must be under-responsive. Mothers often attempt to play the role of both mother and father and, when children become older, find it difficult to let go. They take on too much, trying to be both a good mother and a good father. As a result, children assume less and less responsibility as the mother or father takes on more and more. The family discussion becomes particularly helpful in separation as it is used to focus on shared responsibility, on communicating confidence in the children's ability to manage their own problems, co-ordinating schedules, and planning common activities.

Widowed Parents

The sudden death of a parent is a great shock for members of a family, often resulting in considerable grief, guilt, and anger. 'Why did he/she do this to me?' While grief is an appropriate emotion, guilt and anger are not.

It is important for parents to ensure that children do not feel guilty when they are angry. This can be achieved by demonstrating empathy and by focusing the child's thinking in terms of adjusting to the reality of the death and on where the family goes from here. Many children daydream of how they could have prevented the death and even hope that it will be reversed. The fact of the death must be confronted. Rather than dwelling on the past, children should be encouraged to attend the funeral and plans should be drawn up for the future of the family.

It is particularly difficult for children when the mother dies suddenly, leaving the father who has not developed particular skills with, or interest in, children. Often a father will want to send the children out to be cared for by relatives or will move to a different neighbourhood. Both practices are undesirable as they simply add to the children's problems. In times of upset, children should be kept in an atmosphere which is familiar to them. Further, the father should use the death as an opportunity for teaching children independence at an earlier age, to teach that children have an opportunity of contributing to the family rather than simply being waited on. In all adversity, the opportunity for learning should not be overlooked.

It is likely in the case of a death or a separation that a parent who is taking care of the children will have the desire for a relationship with a member of the opposite sex. Children should be prepared for this eventuality by the parent having regular weekly time to him/herself, time which can later be used for dating. It is, however, undesirable that the remaining parent commence dating too soon after the spouse's death. 'Having lost one parent, am I going to lose another?' While some children may be resentful of the parent dating and accuse the parent of being unfaithful to the dead partner, be not impressed with such a view but teach children that parents have a need for company and that children can help rather than hinder.

The guilt feelings which children are able to create in separated, divorced or widowed parents must be strongly resisted by parents else they become totally controlled by their children and their lives become narrowly focused. One particular separated mother who is known to the author has a 10-year-old daughter. Mother allows the daughter to sleep with her, does her homework with or for her and limits her own leisure activities to those involving the daughter. Her reason? Guilt! 'Might the separation result in my daughter's needs being neglected? I must do as much as I can for her.'

The ability of a family to re-adjust following a death of a parent in terms of financial, social and emotional problems is always a test of the relationship established between parents and children. When those relationships are based on respect, equality, encouragement and trust, there is little to be concerned with in terms of the effects which the loss of a parent will have on the children. Of course, the loneliness, frustration, guilt and ambivalence of the remaining parent are problems which need to be worked through by the family.

Other Types of Single-parent Families

Other types of single-parent families include adopting parents, never-married parents and separated but not divorced parents. The problems facing these parents are not dissimilar to the problems of other single parents and, in time, become similar to the two-parent families.

With the never-married parent, the issue of guilt becomes significant, particularly with unmarried fathers. While traditionally unacceptable to society, this attitude is changing and an ever-increasing number of unmarried mothers are deciding to keep their children. While such mothers have greater financial problems than other single parents, the unmarried father has the problem of guilt in that he is unsure of his responsibilities or how to discharge them. This is a relatively unexplored area but recognises that a person who frequently feels guilty has not the slightest intention of changing. Guilt feelings focus on the past and are concerned with the negative feeling one has about oneself. There is no future orientation concerning what might be done about the event which evokes the feeling of guilt. The good intentions which are associated with guilt feelings are a smoke screen for avoiding doing what an individual knows to be responsible behaviour. The purpose of guilt feelings is to avoid responsible actions.

The basic difference between the separated parent and the divorced parent is that the separated mother finds herself in a vacuum as she is neither single nor married, and not legally free to marry again. Children in a separated marriage have an additional problem as separation usually occurs suddenly and the parent's absence is difficult to understand. Not knowing the reasons for the separation nor having been prepared for it, children will often feel that they have been abandoned and are at a loss to explain the absent parent. As with divorce, children should be prepared for the separation before it happens rather than after the event. Failure to do that only creates anger, guilt, frustration and humiliation in the children.

Summary

In summary, the problems initially faced by single parents are related to the event which led to their current status. In time, however, the problems of the single parent become more like those of two-parent families.

Adults can overcome the initial problem facing children by:
- preparing children for the event if possible;
- recognising the purpose of emotions such as anger, guilt, and fear;
- focusing on the future rather than on the past;
- maintaining the stable environment of the child as far as possible;
- helping the child with relationships with others rather than attempting to control the relationships;
- avoiding the damaging emotion of pity;
- using the event which created the single-parent family as an opportunity for helping children to develop a greater sense of responsibility;
- respecting the former spouse in case of separation or divorce.

Try these

(1) Nine-year-old David, after returning from a weekend with his father, told his divorced mother that his father had said unpleasant things about his ex-wife and had taken David to a most unsuitable and boring social event.

Mother should:

(a) Ring the father and request that he not say nasty things about her and that he should consider activities which were more suitable for David.

(b) Help David cope with the father who makes unpleasant statements or takes him to unsuitable activities.

(2) Mother and father are considering a divorce. The major problem between them is the unfaithfulness of the father. In explaining the situation to her seven-year-old daughter, mother should:

(a) Explain that the relationship between mother and father is not working.

(b) Explain that the behaviour of her husband is creating the problem.

(3) After twelve years of marriage, a mother is killed in a motor accident. Which expression of emotion by the father would be most helpful for the six-year-old son?

(a) 'You poor child . . . What a terrible thing to happen to you at such a young age.'

(b) 'This is a tragic event to have happened but we will cope with it.'

(4) A widow of two years has begun to socialise with another man. Her eight-year-old son says to her: 'I do not like that man you are going out with.' How might mother respond?

(a) 'I will choose my own company without your assistance, thank you.'

(b) 'I am sorry that you do not care for David at present but I hope you will soon.'

(5) How might a father respond to this outburst by his 16-year-old daughter: 'If you had been at home more often, Mum wouldn't have gone off and left us.'?

(a) 'You sound pretty angry about what has happened.'

(b) 'I don't think what I do and don't do is any concern of yours.'

Answers

(1) (b) Mother has no right to tell father how he should behave. Rather than interfere in the relationship between father and his son, mother should help the son get on better with his father.

(2) (a) Children should be taught to understand that a divorce does not imply that either parent is inadequate but rather that the relationship is not working out. The child's parents are not in question but the relationship is faulty.

(3) (b) Show sympathy rather than pity. Pity concentrates on the child while sympathy concentrates on the event and what can be done about it. Pity is a *most* damaging emotion as it erodes the child's confidence at a time when courage is needed.

(4) (b) The issue is not the new partner but the desire by the child to dominate the mother. Mother wisely refuses to be involved in a power contest.

(5) (a) Father refused to be involved in a conflict. The child generated the emotion of anger in order to achieve a purpose. Father, rather than falling for the trap set, used 'reflective listening' and indicated his willingness to discuss the problem and understand the daughter's anger with the separation.

10
Concluding Remarks

Since the first edition of *Becoming Better Parents* was printed in 1981, the great social changes referred to at that time have continued apace. Certain aspects of social change have created more difficulties than others and two areas appear to be particularly significant: the single-parent family and the problems of adolescents. These two areas have been discussed in previous chapters.

The growth of the single-parent family is a recent phenomenon which is likely to continue. In recent years, a virtual society of single-parent families has formed. Following the domestic upheavals of the 1970s when almost one of every two marriages broke apart, the divorce rate has levelled in the 1980s. However, the marital devastation has already been great and the impact on children has worried many people.

With over half the adult female population in the labour force, the rapid collapse of the traditional family which will result in half of the children born in the 1980s spending part of their childhood with one parent, as well as the worsening economic position for many, it is likely that the traditional parent-child conflict will heighten and throw into question the ability of many parents to successfully raise their children.

It is suggested in this book that families headed by single parents can be as psychologically stable as those headed by two parents. It is not an accurate reflection of most events to refer to single-parent homes as 'broken homes'; rather they are alternative family systems in which the relationship between parent and child and the child rearing techniques employed are no different from those that are appropriate to two-parent families. While the particular circumstance which created the single-parent status is the initial problem, the passage of time will result in single-parent families becoming more like traditional families in terms of problems faced.

The behaviour of adolescents has caused concern in many people. In recent years, we have witnessed a spate of violent behaviour by a number of individuals, particularly adolescents. Brutal murders, armed violence, theft, destruction of property, driving offences, alcoholism, crowd brawls, drug abuse, cruelty to animals and arson are just some of the crimes.

Young people have gained freedom without a concomitant sense of responsibility and many of them live in anarchy. Being no longer forced to submit to authoritarian demands, yet deprived of opportunities for developing a sense of responsibility, young people believe that while they have a right to freedom they are not required to accept order.

We must recognise how deeply our young people are involved in a war with the whole generation of adults. It is not only the obvious violent, vicious and delinquent individuals who are involved, but the vast majority of young people. If the solution was simply a matter of good parental example and guidance, we would not find so many irresponsible children coming from responsible homes. No family is secure against the possibility of its youngsters joining the army of active rebels.

The answer to the problem of the difficult adolescent is clearly prevention and it is recommended that parent education is the major solution to counteract problems currently concerning the adolescent. By applying the techniques suggested in this book when children are young, parents can prevent most of the current problems.

It is interesting to observe that the problems which parents have in raising children in this country are no different from those which parents in other countries experience. The problem is that they have no tradition for raising children in the democratic society which radically altered the traditional parent-child relationship. The necessity to live with one another as social equals requires a new set of principles, principles which respect the right of each individual. It serves no purpose to blame parents for the problems children are experiencing.

The majority of parents are vitally concerned in raising responsible individuals but they recognise that the traditional techniques for doing so have lost their effectiveness. They are uncertain.

Considerable experience in working with parents in a variety of situations has convinced me that the principles discussed in this publication can be acquired fairly readily, applied without too much difficulty, and can produce a major improvement in parent-child relationships. While parents can learn the principles themselves, the opportunity for learning and discussing them with others is a decided advantage.

The perfect parent has never existed and never will. We do not aim at perfection but at improvement. In our day-by-day family living, we would like our relationship with each other to be pleasant and stimulating. We do not wish to dominate our children in order to produce mirror images of the types of persons we are or would like to be. We respect the uniqueness of individuals and attempt to foster and encourage their development.

References

Adler, A. *The Practice and Theory of Individual Psychology*. New York: Harcourt, Brace and Co., 1927.

Adler, A. *The Education of Children*. Indiana, Gateway, 1930.

Adler, A. *Understanding Human Behaviour*. New York: Fawcett, 1957.

Ansbacher, H. 'Alfred Adler, Individual Psychology', *Psychology Today*, 1970, 3 (9), 44.

Baruth, L.G. *A Single Parent's Survival Guide*. Iowa, Kendall Hunt, 1979.

Bloom, B.S. *Human Characteristics and School Learning*. New York: McGraw-Hill, 1976.

Dinkmeyer, D. and McKay, G.D. *Step/Teen*. Minnesota, American Guidance Service, 1983.

Dreikurs, R. *The Courage to be Imperfect*. Chicago: Alfred Adler Institute, n.d.

Dreikurs, R. *Social Equality*. Chicago: Henry Regnery, 1971.

Dreikurs, R. and Grey, L. *Logical Consequence*. New York: Meredith, 1968.

Dreikurs, R. *A Parent's Guide to Child Discipline*. New York: Hawthorn Books, 1970.

Dreikurs, R. 'The Psychological Interview in Medicine', *American Journal of Individual Psychology*, Vol.10, 1954, pp.99–122.

Dreikurs, R. 'Technology of Conflict Resolution', *American Journal of Individual Psychology*, Vol.28, 1972, pp.203–206.

Dreikurs, R. *Fundamentals of Adlerian Psychology*. Chicago, Alfred Adler Institute, 1953.

Ferguson, E.D. *Adlerian Theory: an Introduction*. Vancouver, Adlerian Psychology Association of British Columbia, 1984.

Manaster, G. and Corsini, R. *Individual Psychology*. Illinois, Peacock, 1982.

Pepper, F. *The Characteristics of the Family Constellation*. Chicago: Adler Institute, n.d.

Sweeney, T.J. *Adlerian Counseling*. Boston: Houghton Mifflin, 1975.